T0353715

OTHER BOOKS
Presented by Claudia Helt

Seeking A Better Me!
2023

Listen Carefully, Please!
2022

What Awaits Us...
2022

Love Thy Neighbor
2021

Seeking Our Humanity, Part III
2021

Seeking Our Humanity, Part II
2021

Seeking Our Humanity
2021

The Answer in Action
2019

The Answer Illuminated
2019

The Answer
2018

The Time When Time
No Longer Matters
...Continues...
2018

The Time When Time
No Longer Matters
2016

The Book of Ages
2016

Messages from Within:
A Time for Hope
2011

Messages From The Light:
Inspirational Guidance for Light
Workers, Healers, & Spiritual Seekers
2008

The
Power
of
Thoughts

... The Need
for Change ...

Claudia Helt

BALBOA.PRESS
A DIVISION OF HAY HOUSE

Balboa Press books may be ordered through booksellers or by contacting:

Balboa Press
A Division of Hay House
1663 Liberty Drive
Bloomington, IN 47403
www.balboapress.com
844-682-1282

Print information available on the last page.

ISBN: 979-8-7652-5850-7 (sc)
ISBN: 979-8-7652-5849-1 (e)

Library of Congress Control Number: 2024926326

Balboa Press rev. date: 12/19/2024

An Invitation

Welcome, Dear Reader! Once again, you have crossed paths with another opportunity for discovering more about the Self Within. The Self Within, more commonly known as 'You' is a magnificent wonder that encompasses more potential than You have allowed yourself to imagine. The time is now, Dear Friend, for you to discover who you really are.

For those of you who frequently read inspirational books, you are acutely aware of the phrase, 'The Time is Now.' And most likely you are also acquainted with the equally repetitious phrase, 'You are More than You appear to be.' Dear Friend, truths are repeated repeatedly. Perhaps you wonder why messages such as these have been so persistently presented throughout the ages. If you haven't thought about this, now is the time to do so. And if you have thought about it, but haven't come up with an answer, then think about it again, please.

While attempting to provide clarity regarding this mysterious and somewhat annoying process, I must resort to utilizing another often-repeated message. 'This is happening for a reason!' Dear Reader, some messages are so important that they must be repeated over and over again, because the intended recipient fails to recognize ownership of the message. Once again, you have encountered a message urging you to discover more about the Self Within! And you are encouraged to pursue this endeavor now because The Time is Now! Dear Reader, this is happening for a reason!

The Power of Thoughts is an invitation for you to explore more deeply the expansive nature of 'You.' Regardless of your present state of mind, whether you are uplifted, confused, happy, downtrodden, curious, or disinterested, now is the time to take the next step. What that step may be is entirely up to you. However, remember you are more than you appear to be. Why not appropriate time to discover what this curious message means? Explore who you are and discover how you can create changes to become the 'more' you wish, and are intended, to be. *The Power of Thoughts* has crossed your path for a reason. Please accept it as the message it is intended to be. It was created to assist those who desire to know more about the Self yet to be discovered. Enjoy the journey, Dear Reader. Adapt to your discoveries, rest when necessary, and then, repeat the process over and over again. In peace be!

Part One

Discovering the Power of Your Mind

Chapter One

*W*elcome, Dear Reader, and thank you for accepting the invitation to explore and discern more about the beautiful person you really are. Yes, you read the first sentence correctly. You are the beautiful person who is being discussed. Whether you agree with the description or not, the first truth revealed through *The Power of Thoughts* is the reality of your 'Beautiful Self.'

Because the focus of this book targets the thoughts that humans experience, you have an opportunity now, in this moment, to notice what your thoughts are. How is your mind responding to the declaration that you are a beautiful person? Pay attention to your present thoughts and quickly jot them down. You may find it beneficial to make wee reminders for later review as you begin studying the antics of your mind and the thoughts that are created.

Dear Reader, take a deep breath. We just engaged with the initial two paragraphs of *The Power of Thoughts,* and already you have been given 'orders.' Pay attention to your thoughts! Take notes! Take a deep breath! Yikes!

Let's just be together for a moment. Let's relax and enjoy several deep breaths. We deserve it! You and I are walking very similar paths. As you read the words regarding your Beautiful Self for the first time, you probably had many reactions to the presumptuous so-called truth. Personally, I had many thoughts when I first received the words that you just read. "Beautiful person…bah! Nonsense!" Rest assured many of my thoughts were much more critical than those just shared. And of course, my thoughts about the rest of the book yet to come were very dubious.

I silently screamed, "Please, don't let this be another self-help book! Does the world really need another SELF-HELP BOOK?" And of course, the answer was yes! We need all the help we can get. So, the truth is, Dear Reader, when I received the announcement regarding the Beautiful Self, I had to stop and take numerous deep breaths. While doing so, I remembered my years as a Psychotherapist and the many times when I urged a client to take a deep breath. I also remembered the times when I invited clients not to believe everything they thought. Then I remembered how often my own thoughts confused and misled me. And then a smile came to my face.

Occasionally, we must remind ourselves of what we have already learned during our present life cycle. Think about this when you have some time, Dear Reader. You may be surprised. You may discover that you really are a Beautiful Person, and you may also realize that there is more you wish to be. The more you think about the possibilities that remain available to you, the greater understanding you will gain regarding who you are now in this moment, as well as, who you may wish to become from this point forward.

Because humans are a very busy species, our lives are all-consuming. Many of the countless experiences in which we participate daily can go by without our notice. Whether we are vaguely engaged or highly focused on an activity, often there is something missing. Even though we are physically present while attending whatever task is before us, something is missing. The missing component, Dear Reader, is your mind. While you scurry about doing this and that, your mind is elsewhere. Unfortunately, this is a common occurrence. Because we frequently are not present in the moment, we are not consciously aware of our activities. Who knows how much of our lives we are missing? We will not be able to answer that question until we become consistently, consciously present.

Recognizing and accepting the antics of the mind is essential in understanding the power and influence of our thoughts. Opening our hearts to gathering more information about our current thought processes will enable us to grasp the impact that these thoughts are having upon us now, in this moment. In so doing, we will gain greater awareness and understanding of who we really are.

Dear Reader, take another deep breath. You, the other readers of *The Power of Thoughts,* and I are all in need of special attention. We deserve it! And we will definitely benefit from the dedicated time that we give to ourselves.

So, let's move forward together. Let's agree to accept another self-help book into our lives and let's gently, kindly, and carefully proceed with appreciation for Self, for each other, and for the process that we are willingly embarking upon.

Enjoy another satisfying deep breath, Dear Friend. The Beautiful Self that resides within you is yours to discover. Please open your heart to this opportunity. Just imagine meeting your Beautiful Self for the first time. Imagine the fullness of your Beautiful Self. What an incredible Being you are! Please join me in this adventure. Please say yes!

Chapter Two

*D*ear Reader, the time is now. Yes, once again the message of old is repeated, and it is done so for a reason.

Please give a moment to simply be with this new book that you purchased. Hold it to your chest and ask yourself, "Why did I buy this book? What was I thinking when I bought this book? What was I hoping to gain from reading it? Hold on to these questions. They deserve your attention!

However, if your mind continues to generate other questions such as these:

- Is this book really worth my time?
- Have I once again purchased another book that is going to become a dust catcher along with the other forgotten and unread books?
- Do I really need to read this book?
- Is it really going to change my life?

Please notice what your mind is doing!

It is highly probable that your mind is distracting you from the previous questions that are important for you to consider. Let's be realistic! At this point in time, you do not have answers to these distracting questions. You haven't read the book yet, so you don't know if it is going to be life-changing or a waste of time. Address the questions that are relevant, not those that are taking you down illusionary paths of discontentment.

Situations, such as this one, are great opportunities for you to learn more about the workings of your mind. In one moment, questions are posed that will engage you in discovering your Self Within, but before you have time to engage with these meaningful questions, the mind pummels you with more questions, distracting you from your original intention. The initial questions were founded in curiosity, possibilities, open-heartedness, and hopefulness, whereas the distracting questions were suspicious, doubtful, and dismissive. The point being, in a brief moment of time you shifted from an optimistic demeanor to one that is skeptical.

Let's face it, Dear Reader, you purchased *The Power of Thoughts* for a reason. Some part of you hoped, or at least cautiously hoped, that the book may have some answer that might help you improve your present situation. **Please trust that initial reaction.** It happened for a reason. There were other books that may have grabbed your attention, but for whatever reason, this one captured you. Again, you are encouraged to trust your reaction.

Notice what transpired from the time this book entered your range of awareness until you decided to purchase it, and to the moment of reading this chapter. Review the behavior of your mind. Has it been serving you or has it been distracting you?

Take advantage of this situation to learn more about the thoughts your mind generates. If your personal scenario is different from the one just offered, then please utilize your own experience. For instance, if one of your Dear Friends gifted you this book, then how do you feel about receiving a book that you may or may not want. Regardless of the circumstance that brought you and the book together, take notice of the thoughts your mind is having about this union.

Utilize the opportunity to discover more about the part of your mind that misleads your optimistic inclinations. The power of our thoughts is stunning. Our spirits can be lifted in an instant and turned upside down just as quickly. Why and how does this happen? Hopefully, this question piques your curiosity, because it is time for you to discover the underlying mysteries of your mind. In so doing, you will take command of your mind.

Take time, Dear Reader, for a deep breath. There is more to be said before ending this chapter, but a moment of respite is deserved. Count your breaths if you so desire. It may help you discern how many breaths you require to regain your sense of serenity and stillness.

When you feel ready, let us return to the initial questions that were relevant to your first encounter with *The Power of Thoughts.*

- Why did I buy this book?
- What was I thinking when I bought this book?
- What was I hoping to gain from reading it?

These questions deserve your consideration. Please attempt to remember what was going on with you when you encountered the book for the first time. Try to recapture the feelings you had about reading the book. Did you feel drawn to the book as if somehow it was reaching out to you, trying to get your attention? Listen now with the ears of your heart. Attempt to reconnect with that energy. Allow it to reignite your desire and willingness to open your heart to the possibilities that may be awakened by participating in this reading experience.

The energy that coaxed you in this direction still exists, and it will become more accessible as you enhance your habits of openhearted connectedness.

Dear Reader, there is a reason for this review of your first experience with *The Power of Thoughts*. As the title states, this book is about thoughts. We begin our research into the mystery of your thoughts by accessing and utilizing the experience of your first encounter with the book as a model for how we will proceed in our study of the power of thoughts.

Chapter Three

Time for Silence…

*D*ear Reader, you are invited to begin a new adventure into the realm of Silence. If this is your first excursion into the Silence, be patient with the process, and have compassion for yourself while you adapt to this new experience. If you are one who visits the Silence on a regular basis, please remember that every adventure is different. Experience reminds you that it is wise to embrace patience and compassion as amiable companions during the adventure. Eventually, each of you will learn and graciously accept that these two gentle traits are essential to the journey within.

Whether you are a novice or a devoted seeker of the Silence, this exercise is an opportunity for you to embrace an adventure. If you are wondering why a new Chapter is beginning in this way, the answer is simple. The time is now!

So, join me now please, and let's experience a moment of Silence. Our goal for this exercise is brief, only five minutes; however, if you wish to enjoy a longer time with the Silence, please do what best suits you.

Breathe deeply and gently. Find a pace that is comfortable for you and release all thoughts, as best you can, as you settle into the realm of Silence.

Listen to your Breath.
Listen to the Silence.
Simply be in the Silence.

When ending your time in the silence, enjoy one more deep breath and then return to the present. If time allows, record the experience you just had. If other obligations are calling, then make very brief notes so that you can continue to explore this adventure at a later time. Whether you address the experience immediately or later, is yours to discern, but please follow through. Dedicate time for reviewing, pondering, opening, and accepting your adventure into the Silence.

As annoying as it may seem, there is a reason for recording your experiences in the Silence. Actually, there are many reasons, but the first one that comes to mind is the reality that what you experience in the Silence has a high propensity for being forgotten. With time, one can and does become more skillful at remembering what transpires during the inward experience; however, in the beginning stages of your exploration process, your willingness to accept the importance of jotting down brief notes will enable the process to move along more smoothly.

Dear Ones, another thought comes to mind. It is not uncommon for individuals to speak about the difficulty of the inward journey. Indeed, it can be frustrating at times; nevertheless, every moment spent engaging and participating with the act of moving inward is a precious opportunity for expansion.

Is the process difficult? Some would say 'Yes!' Maybe you are one who can attest to the complexities of the inward journey. Regardless of your previous experiences or your future experiences, you are encouraged to continue your inward explorations, and you are invited to choose a mindful approach. Rather than presuming that the next experience is going to be complicated, choose to pursue it with an open heart and a curious mind. Welcome the challenges! Please allow me to repeat that statement. WELCOME THE CHALLENGES!

Absorb everything you can from every occurrence you encounter, whether the event is seemingly hindering your journey or accelerating it. Diving deeply within is an exciting adventure, if you allow yourself to embrace each encounter along the way. While some days may seem like 'a waste of time,' others will leave you overwhelmed with 'fullness.' Whichever side of the continuum you find yourself on, accept it as a gift...a privileged learning opportunity...that will assist you in discovering who you are in that particular moment.

The developmental phase of your exploration practice will be much more pleasant if you choose to proceed with your two new best friends...patience and compassion. Furthermore, you may find it wise to leave self-criticism and negativity behind. Truthfully, exchanging self-criticism and negative inclinations for patience and compassion can be a life-changing decision.

Choose now, Dear Reader, to begin a practice of praising your efforts:

- No matter how large or small the action may be, applaud yourself!
- Appreciate each effort made!
- Regard each step forward or backward equally and accept the effort as more information gained.
- Notice what is happening and express gratitude for your increased knowledge about yourself and about the Silence.

Accepting the importance of these suggestions will assist you with the journey that lies ahead. It is particularly important in the early stages of your exploration process. Exuberant beginners delving into their new practice sometimes mistakenly focus their intentions on the negative aspects of their behavior. Unfortunately, some individuals become overwhelmed during this period and find it difficult to release themselves from that phase of learning. This tendency may be one of the reasons why so many people find these experiences difficult.

Undeniably, we all have issues that need investigation and improvement; however, please consider pursuing a kinder and wiser way of seeking greater understanding. You are more than just the negative issues that surface in the early stages of your journey, Dear Reader, and there are other parts of you that need your attention as well. Balance your work by also focusing upon the goodness within you.

My Dear Friends, with a tender heart and a smile on my face, I offer this suggestion. Please remember that seeking within is not 'all about you!' Experience informs us that when we begin exploring ourselves, we can lose sight of the reality that the inward journey entails much more than just oneself.

Without a doubt self-exploration is a huge endeavor; however, seeking within opens opportunities for expansion that are beyond our imagination. There is a much bigger picture to this process than we are aware of when we begin the journey. Those who have long participated in the inward journey will attest that the more you explore, the more cognizant you are of how little you know. The bigger picture is an ongoing, never-ending testament that "There is More!"

Dear Ones, within the Silence you will learn more about all there is to know, and in so doing, clarity will be gained regarding the enormity of what remains unknown.

At times your inward journey will focus upon you. Other times, your focus will be elsewhere. Sometimes you will sense connection, other times you will not. Sometimes you will feel frustration, other times you may feel exuberance. Each exploration is an unknown that sometimes becomes known and other times remains elusive and mysterious. The possibilities are endless.

Regardless of what transpires, the experience has some type of impact upon you, and your thoughts will certainly play a role in how you process your experiences.

Within you, you will discover the best of you and the worst of you. You may discover parts of you that you would prefer to remain unknown. If and when this transpires, please do not fear the challenge. Instead, greet the moment as an opportunity for growth. Just take a deep breath and move forward knowing that you will not be the only person experiencing this type of discovery.

Life brings us many experiences. One of our many challenges is to quiet the unpleasantness of the past as well as the present. By addressing unpleasant issues, greater understanding of the influence these events had upon you is gained, which in turn releases you from their burden so that you can be free to become your fullest Self in the present moment.

Your exploration may also bring you surprises regarding your essence of goodness. Yes, Dear Reader, you read that correctly…YOUR ESSENCE OF GOODNESS! It's real! And it exists within you!

Occasionally, one gets lost in the sorrows of the so-called 'worst' of self and unfortunately loses track of the 'best' side. Your goodness, your kindness needs as much attention as is given the 'worst' of you. It is essential! Exploring, accepting, and remembering the 'best' part of you is a significant part of the inward journey. Balance must always be sought when exploring the True Self.

Whatever you discover during your journey is yours to manage. You are in charge! Please remember you are exploring 'yourself,' and this is an intimate, private affair. Use patience and compassion throughout this process, including the decisions that must be made regarding with whom you will and will not share your newfound information.

Time for the Curious Mind...

A curious mind can be a remarkable asset throughout your self-discovery process. Energized by the unknown, the curious mind welcomes new information. It delights in every aspect of the discovery process while also accepting responsibility for the manner in which the information is gained.

The curious mind at times seems to be hyperactive, desiring to consume all new information as quickly as possible; however, rapid consumption is not always the best path to take. Fortunately, the curious mind can modulate its desires with appropriate guidance. Dear Reader, you are a remarkable being with remarkable skills. Developing a greater understanding of your curious mind will enhance all aspects of your life in addition to the current inward journey that you are pursuing.

Before moving forward, perhaps it is wise for us to spend some time exploring the curious mind. This exercise will provide you with an opportunity to experience your curious mind in the moment.

Take several deep breaths, please, and allow yourself to engage with the Silence again. Allot a minimum of 5 minutes for this activity. Please do so now.

Listen to your Breath.
Listen to the Silence.
Simply be in the Silence.

After your brief encounter with the Silence, take another deep breath. Your next step is to review your thoughts when you were invited to explore the Silence.

Think back:

- Were you open-hearted about the opportunity?
- Were you curious about what you might learn during this exercise?
- Did you experience excitement or frustration or some other reaction?
- Attempt to recall what you were thinking and why.
- Welcome all reactions that you experienced.

Once again you are advised to make notes. The goal of this exercise is for you to gain better clarity about the workings of your mind.

- How did the thoughts instantaneously generated by your mind influence you?
- How did these thoughts serve you?
- How did these thoughts impede you?
- How might you improve your thought processes?

Thank you, Dear Reader, for participating in this exercise which was intended to provide you with additional information about the workings of your remarkable mind. Hopefully, the time spent observing your mind was fruitful. Recognizing that your mind is always operating, even when you are not paying attention to it, is extremely important information. It is in your best interest to study your mind's daily activities. Unless you are aware of its minute-to-minute interactions, then you are not truly in command of your life.

Through your observations, you will witness your mind's potential and realize how important it is for you to be knowledgeable of its constant activities. The power of your thoughts will become increasingly understood when you give your mind the attention that is needed. Not only will you recognize its potential, but you will also understand the necessity of your role. You are the one who is in command of your life. The mind is not your leader, you are its leader!

Dear Reader, take a deep breath and allow yourself to embrace this reality. You are in command of your life. Take several more long deep breaths and simply be with this truth.

...YOU ARE IN COMMAND OF YOUR LIFE...

Pay attention to your thoughts, as you read your truth in bold letters. Continue to read and re-read this statement of truth, and as you do, listen to the thoughts that are racing through your mind. Please take wee notes as you observe the conversation going on in your remarkable mind. The notes will be incredibly useful for future review, but do not allow your notetaking to distract you from observing your internal conversation.

Your primary task is focusing upon your thoughts:

- What comments are being made about your promotion to commander?
- Are the comments positive thoughts or are they negative?
- Are your thoughts applauding your upgraded status?
- Are your thoughts excited about learning more about your promotion?
- Are 'you' excited about learning more about your new responsibilities?

- Are the comments supportive of your new promotion?
- Are negative comments entering the conversation?
- Are they effecting the mood of the conversation?
- Notice changes in the mood of your thoughts.
- Notice changes in your mood.
- Has your observation of your thought process been beneficial?
- What have you learned?
- Does your mind have a tendency toward an uplifting demeanor, or does it tend to be cautious, reticent to change, and leaning towards the opposite direction of uplifting?

While determining what you have learned, be as gentle with yourself as you would be with a dear friend.

...Be patient. Be kind. Be compassionate...

Please pay particular attention to how you react to any negative thoughts that surfaced during your brief observation. Often there is a tendency to be negative about one's inner negative commentary. This is not uncommon. Most of us have these moments. Consider it another opportunity to recognize what is actually happening in your mind. AND THEN, choose another strategy!

Rather than fussing at yourself for fussing at yourself, instead choose to be as patient, kind, and compassionate as you can possibly be. If you find yourself struggling about this, then take a deep breath, and observe your thoughts again. Accept whatever comes forward.

Recognizing old habits that do not serve us is an unpleasant experience; however, it does not justify another act of negativity. This is not a time for critical judgment. It is a time for change! Witness the negativity, accept that it is part of you, and trust that you have the power to change these habits. In essence, you do have command over your negative thoughts, and you do have the power to alter your current ways.

Time to Celebrate...

Dear Readers, thank you for participating in this chapter. It has been one that offered many opportunities. By now, some of you may once again be thinking, "This definitely is another SELF-HELP BOOK!"

Why wouldn't this thought be racing through your mind? After all, you've been given a long list of orders!

Do this! Do that! Take a deep breath!
Observe your thoughts! Accept your thoughts!
Be patient! Be kind! Be compassionate!
Oh my!

A lot was asked of you throughout this chapter. I hope you benefitted from the opportunity. One's inner work can be intense and tiring...please take good care of you during this process. Rest when it is needed and continue the adventure when you feel it is right to do so. Trust yourself! You know more about 'You' than anyone else does. Take control of your self-discovery process by taking care of you.

Time for the Beautiful Self...

Let me remind you of a truth that was revealed in the first chapter. You are the Beautiful Self you are seeking. During your exploration, parts of you may be revealed that you will wish to improve. This doesn't mean that you are NOT a beautiful person. We are all in transition! With each experience, we learn, we grow, we expand, and our desire to know more about who we really are continues.

The Beautiful Self is like a budding flower. Each day another blossom appears, and the beautiful flower is more than the day before. Likewise, each lesson you experience adds to the beauty that you already possess. Just as the flower sheds leaves and blooms that no longer serve, so too do you shed that which is no longer helpful to your Beautiful Self. This is who you are... an ever-changing, ever-expanding Beautiful Being.

The challenges that are presented throughout this book are intended to help you discover more about the Beautiful Being that you are, while also helping you to understand that some of what you have already learned is now ready to be released.

Dear Reader, be patient, be kind, and be compassionate with your Beautiful Self!

Today is the last day of your life as you now know it, and tomorrow is the first day of the rest of your everlasting life. Enjoy this day to the fullest and prepare to do the same tomorrow. Cherish each moment, regardless of its tenor. Every experience, even those that are unexpected and undesirable offer you an opportunity to learn more about your Beautiful Self.

Chapter Four

*I*n the previous chapter, Dear Readers, you were introduced to the amazing power of your thoughts. Hopefully, each of you gained greater awareness of the capabilities of your mind. Some of you may be shocked by the inner workings of the mind. If this is the case, please be at ease. You have made a very important discovery! You now know it is in your best interest to be alert to the antics of your mind. For instance, be attentive to your remarkable mind now and see that it doesn't interfere with our current conversation.

This is a time for all the Readers presently engaged with this book to accept the reality that you are exactly where you need to be. To gain command of your Life, it is essential that you become the leader of your mind. Whether you were previously aware of this information or not is irrelevant. What is wonderful is that each one of you is learning or re-learning about it now! Suffice it to say, the power of the mind is tenacious, and it is wise to remember that it will continue to challenge you for the leadership role that it so cherishes.

This is your opportunity to gain a firmer grip upon the role of leadership that is yours to master. Actually, it is your moment to create greater vitality in your future. When the mind learns to cooperate with you and your intentions, you will experience a new level of functioning. Over time you will enjoy more confidence while also feeling a greater sense of peace. Your increased productivity will delight you as you witness it transpiring quicker, easier, and more efficiently. Life will be less chaotic and less stressful.

Initially, you may be reluctant to trust the changes that are unfolding, but go ahead and take a leap! Accept that your life has changed! And more importantly, accept that you orchestrated these changes by educating your mind to work with you. The capabilities that the mind exhibits are remarkable and unbelievable! And with your leadership it becomes even more impressive. Express gratitude, Dear Readers, for the blessing that you were gifted!

Each of you will have your own individual experiences with your powerful mind. Stand firm! Be flexible! Practice various approaches! Continue practicing! And as always, be patient, kind, and compassionate.

Another thought comes to mind. Remember you are not alone in this challenge to monitor the mind that has had its own way for a very long time. Send inspirational thoughts, words of encouragement, and visualizations of applause to your reading companions across the planet. Also share some of your energy with each other so that all of you are giving and receiving positive energy as you welcome your remarkable mind to a new way of being. Once the mind understands that it has much more potential when working in union with its beholder, the process unfolds effortlessly.

Perhaps some of you are confused about our discussion regarding the mind. If this is your initial reaction, rest assured you are in good company. This is not a topic that is easily addressed. Often there is confusion and misunderstanding about the mind and the human brain. Because we do not wish to get caught up in this confusion, let me acknowledge that this conversation is not about the functioning of the human brain. We are here to learn more about our involvement, or perhaps better said, our lack of involvement with the thoughts of the mind.

Although it may seem ridiculous to think that we are not involved with our thoughts, the point is we are often unaware of the machinations of our highly active mind.

Let's pause for a moment, Dear Friend. Take a deep breath and notice what your mind is up to.

- Is your mind focused on the words in front of you?
- Or is it thinking about another task that must be done?
- Perhaps, it is replaying a conversation recently had or recalling a movie recently seen.
- The point is…**what is your mind thinking about** and is it in alignment with your perception of what you are presently thinking?

Dear Reader, please take another deep breath and open your heart to a conversation with your mind. This may sound odd, but you can do it! Truth is, you have probably done this countless times before, but this time, you will be doing it intentionally. It is time, my Friend, for you and your unruly mind to work on your relationship.

If you are wondering how to proceed with this endeavor, a suggestion that has already been offered several times comes to mind. *Be patient, be kind, and be compassionate with yourself and with your mind. Remember, your mind is a part of you. Treat the mind in the same manner that you would like to be treated.*

The purpose of this exercise is for you to take the lead in establishing a relationship with your mind. A relationship is already in process; however, as with all relationships, attention is necessary for the welfare of all those involved.

Take a few more deep breaths, Dear Friend, and invite your mind to join you in this relaxing exercise.

- Breathing in, invite your intentions and your mind's intentions to merge.
- Breathing out, release the tension between you and within you.
- Continue this breathing exercise until you feel at ease about having this discussion with your mind.
- When ready, begin by expressing your gratitude for everything your mind has done for you. Praise its efforts.
- Then, seek your mind's assistance. Express your need for its cooperation in the tasks that lie ahead. Specifically address the tasks of concern, and sincerely request for a collaborative working relationship.

- Treat your mind as you would treat a Dear Friend.
- Remember that your mind is part of you, and at all times, it deserves your kindness, gentleness, and loving guidance.
- Express your desire for a long and lasting relationship.
- End your exercise with several rewarding deep breaths.

Dear Friends, accept this exercise as a guide for your future relationship with your mind. As stated earlier, your mind is accustomed to being in charge and it will readily step forward to do so again. Over time I've come to believe that being in charge is simply its nature. However, with frequent conversations that are founded in kindness and wisdom, the mind willingly becomes an ardent assistant to you. Attend this relationship with tender care and you will find life so much easier to navigate.

Chapter Five

*N*ow that you are alerted to the tenacity of your mind's desire to be in charge, perhaps this is a good time to explore your attitude about commanding and being responsible for your mind. What I am about to say may seem odd, but there is a difference between your self-generated thoughts and the thoughts that seem to pop up out of nowhere. Unless you are paying attention, i.e., unless you are consciously aware in the moment, it is doubtful that you will even know that you have an issue that needs addressing. To delineate one from the other demands your attention.

Dear Readers, my first awareness of the complexity of my mind occurred longer ago than anyone in his or her right mind would want to admit. And even though I would love to say that I immediately took charge and reined my runaway thoughts into a safe healing chamber, that did not happen! Truthfully, I barely noticed the encounter and went on my merry way as if the incident had never happened.

This is a typical example of someone who experienced a very brief moment of conscious awareness and then quickly returned to her multi-tasking way of being. Like many of you, I too was capable of efficiently juggling numerous tasks at once. I was sharp, competent, very busy, and seemingly very present to those around me. And at the same time, there was part of me that was truly unconscious to the reality of being fully present to that which was going on within and around me.

What about you, Dear Reader? Have you given this concept of being consciously present and aware any attention? Have you thought about it? Have you noticed during your busy day that something is amiss?

The reason I ask is probably obvious by now, but just in case, let me ask a few more questions. As you read the four previous paragraphs, were you totally present to what you were reading? Did you check your emails in between paragraphs, or did you take a quick break to grab a favorite treat? Or maybe you are an early riser and needed to quickly create your daily To Do List between one sentence and the next. Point being, were you able to read the first four paragraphs of this chapter without distraction?

Hopefully, many of you were able to do so! Those of you who achieved what seems to be a simple task deserve applause and numerous pats on the back. Those of you who encountered numerous bouts with distraction during your brief reading experience also deserve applause and pats on the back. I say this with sincerity and gratitude, because the fact that you noticed your wandering mind is an exceptional achievement of conscious awareness. *Applause, applause, applause!*

As is true with most, if not all groups, the Readers of *The Power of Thoughts* will have similarities and differences. Some will have commendable focus, while others will struggle maintaining focus. Some of you will be in a place in your life where the information found in this book is deeply meaningful for you. Others may experience confusion and frustration. The truth is we are all different and each one of us will have our own unique experience with the amazing mind that resides within us.

The beauty of the human species' differences is the massive amount of information that is available due to our individual perspectives. Think about this, please. For every individual, there is an unknown quantity of knowledge that was accumulated, contemplated, internalized, and altered by the beholder's personal interpretation.

...A Time for Thoughts...

Take a deep breath and for a moment allow yourself to imagine what the world would be like if we would learn to accept one another's viewpoints.

- Just imagine what it would be like to open our hearts to the experiences of others.
- Rather than immediately rejecting another's perspective just because it is different, we could listen with an open heart and a curious mind and integrate the richness of another's perspective into our own.
- Imagine how the energy of humankind would shift if we optimistically and graciously opened our minds to accepting one another's differences.

Extend this moment of exploration by envisioning a particular person in your life with whom you would like to discuss this topic.

- Picture you and your selected person in a comfortable setting.
- Picture yourself introducing the topic of the beauty of differences and the abundant knowledge available because of these differences. Envision yourself sharing the ideal of everyone opening her or his heart to the possibility of accepting the perspectives of others.
- What thoughts arise within you when you imagine doing this? Are they uplifting, curious, open-hearted, and excited? Or are your thoughts cautious, worried, and/or hesitant?
- Without judgment, explore the reactions of your thoughts? Learn more about yourself when you imagine being in the company of your chosen person.
- *Choose another person and repeat the exercise.* Again, learn more about your thoughts and yourself when you imagine being in the company of this newly selected person.

As you can see, the flexibility of this exercise can provide you with a tremendous amount of information about YOU. It is also an interesting opportunity for you to practice becoming the person you truly want to be when you are in the company of others. And furthermore, it is a way of testing your mind's thoughts.

One must remember that this is an exercise played out within the mind. What will transpire when you actualize this event with another person is yet to be seen.

Hmm! Another thought just came to mind. Take the next step!

- Imagine sending an email or calling someone to schedule a 'meet up' time to discuss the current topic of the beauty of differences.
- How are you reacting to this challenge?
- How is your mind reacting to this challenge?
- Visit your thoughts and learn from them. Whether they are ecstatic or fearful, or somewhere in between, just be with these thoughts and learn everything you possibly can learn about YOU. Of course, it would be wise to record your thoughts, your deliberations, and your conclusions.
- Applaud yourself for this amazing self-exploratory work!

…A Time to Breathe…

Once you have had some time to breathe, relax, and celebrate your good work, you will, of course, need to take another step…

Oh, Dear One, by now you must be throwing up your hands and screaming internally, "Enough Already!" I would be if I were you.

However, another step really does remain to be taken. I know this is pushy, but just take another deep breath and meet the challenge. Discern whom you wish to invite and follow through with the invitation.

This is an opportunity for your Beautiful Self to engage with another similar, yet different Beautiful Self.

...A Time to Breathe and Reflect...

Rest now, Dear Readers. Take time to breathe and reflect upon the exercises just experienced. Be grateful for what you have done and what you have learned. Allow your mind to ponder about the various thoughts that surfaced during the exercises and notice the reactions that quickly came to mind. Also pay attention to the thoughts and reactions that are still operating now as you review your earlier experiences.

The mind is a remarkable asset, particularly so when you are consciously aware of what it is doing. As said earlier, memory recall can sometimes be an issue when you initially begin your exploratory path. Recording your experiences in whatever way is suitable to you can be extremely beneficial. The act of recording, whether it be by pen, computer, or artwork, often brings greater clarity of what has transpired.

This process gives your mind another opportunity to demonstrate its talent which provides you with more information about its operational ways. The benefits of having some type of journal that you can easily access will be quickly evident.

Chapter Six

Shall we continue? In the previous chapter, numerous opportunities were provided that gave you more opportunities to study your mind. As you pay more attention to the mind, you learn how capable it is, and you also become aware of how ornery it can be.

In essence the mind's capability of multi-tasking is mind-blowing. One would assume that is a positive factor. It certainly was intended to be so; however, over time the mind acquires habits, some of which are extremely positive and serviceable while others are not. Unless you are aware of your mind's operational habits, you will not realize that some of the mind's preferred habits are actually in need of improvement. *Please do not be alarmed by this!* We are a species that is constantly seeking to improve itself. This is just part of the life process.

When approaching my fiftieth year, much to my surprise, my life process took a startling turn. Suddenly, my interests changed. What seemed to be exactly as I desired it to be no longer seemed right. I felt restless and without an anchor to keep me centered and satisfied. Everything previously strived for was achieved and yet, it no longer brought me pleasure. My world just didn't seem right. Perhaps this transition unfolded over time, but if it did, it happened without my notice. One day, everything was as preferred and the next day, something was profoundly different. Something was missing.

What was missing was me! I was so focused on my career that I was missing all the clues that were apprising me that there was "more!" Until that moment, that awakening moment, I was satisfied, happy, and content with my life as a therapist. Working as a therapist was a beautiful period of Grace, a precious time which allowed me to fully enjoy that wonderful life cycle, before the next big life experience unfolded. I realize now that the role as therapist prepared me for the next experience. As a therapist, I was a listener and had the privilege of honing that skill for numerous years before becoming another type of listener.

The book that you are now reading is the result of those new listening skills. This new career was a surprise, and still surprises me to this day. There really is "more" and the books that I have had the privilege to publish are proof of that.

As with the other books received, the title of this book was provided to me about a month before the work began. Because I am not comfortable with surprises, my Companions wisely and lovingly inform me in advance so that I can prepare myself for the next adventure. Preparation means getting the rest of my life in order, so I am free to devote all my time to the next project.

In the past when a new project was announced it brought joy to my heart. I was very excited about being part of the unveiling of a new book. There was, and continues to be, a grace-filled mystery about this process. I show up. I listen. I take dictation. And the words flood the pages. What I am trying to convey, Dear Reader, is that I deeply enjoy my calling. In the beginning it seemed very unusual, but with time it became normal, and at this point, I am accustomed to how smoothly the process unfolds. In truth, I take it for granted. My trust in these experiences is so solid that I was truly taken aback by the unpredictable birthing of this new book.

When apprised of the title of the upcoming book, my reaction was not gracious. (Actually, it was appalling.) My mind immediately assumed it was going to be a Self-Help book and recoiled from the idea. Together, my mind and my Self went down paths of obnoxious resistance, exaggerated dissatisfaction, ridiculous fantasies and judgments about the unknown book's content and then came shame. As said, Dear Reader, my behavior was pitiful, and truthfully, I was relieved when shame entered the scene, because it put a stop to the nonsense. This was a shocking experience for me.

So, what happened? Receiving these messages is my calling. I've devoted over two decades of my life to this process, and I am acutely aware of, and grateful for, the privilege of serving in this way. Why did I react in such a petulant manner? Who am I to question this new endeavor? Who am I to reject such an incredible opportunity?

As you might imagine, revealing my misguided behavior to anyone, much less the Readers of this book is not something that I want to do. It's embarrassing! However, important information may be gained from this uncomfortable situation. Obviously, this is an opportunity for self-exploration. If I choose to avoid doing the inner work that is needed regarding this incident, there may be a similar event again in the future. Why would anyone want to repeat this experience? Instead, it makes sense to do the work now and hopefully gain new insights about my recent behavior.

Dear Reader, as we discussed earlier, there is so much information available that can be gained by studying others' perspectives. Please take advantage of my recent unpleasant experience and learn from my mistakes. Ponder why I reacted the way I did. Put yourself in my shoes.

- How would you handle the situation?
- How would you help me recover from the experience?
- How would you offer support to me?
- How would you want to be assisted through a similar experience?

If the previous questions take you to a scenario of your own, then address your personal issue instead. Hopefully, we will all gain new skills that will assist us in becoming more equipped in facing our own experiences while also discovering how to assist others through their situations.

So here we go, Dear Friends. Four paragraphs ago, reality slapped me in the face. After acknowledging my embarrassment about sharing my misguided behavior, I knew it was time to take action. A choice was involved. I could either deny what had happened and hope that it never happened again, or I could face what had happened, learn from it, and hopefully improve myself with the knowledge gained.

Please remember that your experience of reading the paragraph for the first time was similar to my receiving it in the moment. My mind was actively involved with the options. Here's a list of some of my thoughts:

- I do not want to share my outrageous behavior with anyone. It's private!
- I do not want to relive this experience by exploring it up one side and down the other.
- I do not want to behave like this again.
- I cannot refuse to do this inner work. It must be done.
- I cannot allow myself to behave in this way again.
- Do the right thing, Claudia!

As you can see, the mind and I traveled from a defensive posture to a rational posture to an honorable posture, and it did so in a relatively brief amount of time. The first two declarations which were founded in fear were the hardest to release. I think it is fair to say that most of us have memories of behavioral incidents that we would prefer to remain a secret. In some circumstances wisdom advises us to remain silent. However, other incidents deserve a discernment process: a time to ponder the reality of revealing information that you fear may harm you or another. In this situation, I was embarrassed and ashamed of my behavior. At first, I couldn't imagine sharing this story. Nor did I want to dwell in this muck while exploring my inner intentions.

And then a rational side of me came into play. Rather than focusing on negative possibilities, the sensible part of me questioned what would really happen if others found out about my petulant behavior.

- Would I lose friends?
- Would I become an outcast?
- Would I be condemned to wear a "Petulant Woman" T-shirt for the rest of my life?

Not likely! All those thoughts that pop up out of nowhere need a second look. **Do not believe everything you think!** Some thoughts may surface that deserve more attention, and by all means give those the attention that is needed. But do not allow thoughts to aimlessly lead you around in circles of confusion.

Clearly, the part of me that wanted to avoid doing the inner work needed more attention. My initial response was the equivalent of a knee jerk reaction. In the moment, I did not want to do the work! However, the truth is I'm one of those people who embraces self-discovery. I have a great deal of experience doing this type of exploration; nevertheless, when the avoidance thoughts popped up, they had impact. Fortunately, in this scenario the thoughts were not tenable enough to take the lead. Had I not been aware of the activity of my thoughts, they would have had much more influence. This is where conscious awareness comes into play. **If you are not aware of what your mind is doing, then you are not in command of your life.**

Dear Readers, if I could turn back time and relive that experience, there are things that I would do differently. For instance, when I was presented the new book title, I wish:

- I had said, "Thank You!" Thank you for allowing me to participate in this incredible work. I look forward to collaborating with you again, and I am eager to get started.
- I had just sat quietly embracing the reality that another book was being birthed.
- I had remembered what a privilege it was to be part of this process.

And when my reaction to the title of the book instantaneously went sour, I wish I had taken several deep breaths to calm myself and counteract the nonsense of my mind. I wish I had asked:

- Why are you jumping to conclusions based upon nothing more than a book title?
- Why are you resistant to receiving a Self-Help Book?
- Why are you reacting this way?
- Why are you behaving so disrespectfully?
- Have you forgotten your calling?
- Why don't you ask your Companions to assist you in understanding what is going on with you?

"Dear Readers, because of the refined listening skills of our Dear Friend, Claudia, we are able to communicate

with you at this time. She currently is squirming in her chair because she is surprised by our desire to connect with you directly. Even though she has delivered messages for us to many, many people around the world, she still feels self-conscious about this remarkable process.

We are the Ones that Claudia refers to as her Companions, and we announce ourselves for several reasons. First and foremost, our intentions are to assist humankind with their efforts to create peace on the Life Being Earth. Peace is possible! It is not a dream or a wishful thought; it is a necessity that requires immediate attention by all inhabitants of the planet. The non-humans residing on the planet are already acutely aware of the planet's difficult situation. Species of all kinds strive to help Mother Earth. These neighbors who co-exist with the human species are already working to create a better environment. But they cannot heal the planet on their own. The task to save the Earth demands everyone to be involved. All are needed. No species is excluded from this responsibility.

Although many non-human species are attempting to communicate with their human neighbors, very few attempts are successful. Hopefully, in the near future that situation will change. As discussed earlier, the perspectives of others are a valuable source of knowledge. While humans struggle to accept this concept within their own species, they must also accept this reality among all other species. Collaboration among all species is the most expedient and efficient way of correcting the Earth's declining situation.

Dear Readers, we are aware that our presence may be a surprise to you. We do not wish to cause confusion.

Our desire is to gain your trust by connecting with you through the pages of this book. We too have important information from which your species can benefit. We are another species that you would be wise to engage with.

Our Dear Friend, the Life Being Earth, is loved and cherished by all other Life Beings in existence. She is revered and held in the highest regard. Mother Earth is our primary reason for reaching out to you in this unusual manner. Her health is rapidly declining. Her symptoms are obvious. No longer can anyone pretend that the changes transpiring across the globe are of no consequences.

The Earth cannot survive without the help of the human species. And your species cannot manage this unfolding catastrophe without the assistances of others. Although your species has prided itself for its individualism, you will not succeed in altering what is transpiring unless you seek help from others. We intend no disrespect to your remarkable species, nevertheless, the truth must be bluntly spoken. Your survival is dependent upon the presence of a healthy, flourishing planet. Mother Earth needs assistance now! You need assistance now!

Our most heartfelt desire is that you will allow us to be your Companions in this mission to Save the Earth. Although our method of reaching out to you may seem unusual, please give us the opportunity to win your trust. We are not strangers. We have been your Companions since you came into existence. Only a few of you see us and/or hear us, but all of you have the ability to do so. This too probably sounds unusual. We hold all your reactions in our hearts, and we understand that this is an extremely puzzling experience. We mean no harm. Please remember this. Our desire is to help, not to harm. We seek your permission to be of assistance."

Well, that was an unexpected surprise! Dear Readers, I am trying to imagine what you are feeling at this moment. I wonder how you are doing. Please take several deep breaths, as many as are needed, and try to compose yourself after receiving the Message from the Companions. If I were you, there would be many, many thoughts racing through my mind. Truthfully, my own thoughts are currently moving at Olympic speed. Those of you who have had unusual experiences such as this one before are probably having similar thoughts to mine. Like me, you may be concerned for those who have not yet had such an experience. I so wish we could all sit together and talk through this curious event. Sharing our stories would be very beneficial. I still remember what it was like when the communications with the Companions first began. It was overwhelmingly exciting, but at the time, there was no one with whom I could discuss the encounters. So, the excitement was accompanied by loneliness.

Even though the Companions were near, I couldn't see them. Yes, I could hear them and that was remarkable, but doubts surfaced. Is this real? Can it really be happening? I'm hearing voices…am I diagnosable? You name it and I thought it.

It took a while for me to adjust to the reality that what was happening was real. The messages received were beautiful, loving, and kind, and way beyond my scope of imagination. And never once did I hear words that were not founded in goodness. At one point I remember thinking, "If this is crazy, then bring it on!" I knew in that moment that whatever was happening was real and I was not going to turn my back on the opportunity being given to me. Just because I couldn't see the Companions and didn't fully understand the situation didn't mean it wasn't real.

It takes time to grasp this new reality. I still have doubts occasionally, but the messages, the books received, and all the incredible experiences that I have had cannot be tossed aside because of a moment of doubt. I do not regret one moment of the last twenty plus years living in connection with the Companions. They are real! Someday, I would love to see them with my human eyes, but it isn't necessary. I feel their presence, I trust their guidance, and I am stunned by their compassion and kindness for All Beings.

Life was good before I was aware of the Companions, but life is so much better since I became involved with them. Gratitude is always present within me and that changes one's perspective of life and the world with which one co-exists.

Dear Ones, I hope you will give yourself time to digest what you just read and experienced. This is a time for you to breathe, pay attention to your thoughts, observe your feelings, and take a lot of notes. Particularly, those of you who are newcomers to such an experience, please take notes. Try to remember every thought, reaction, doubt, feeling, fear, excitement, etc. that you can remember. It is important to do so. Even though you have the book and can reread the Companion's message whenever you desire, it is still important to record everything you can remember as quickly as you can.

If you sense urgency in my request, you are intuiting correctly. I urge you to record your experiences, because your initial thoughts and reactions are so valuable. This is where you find the most accurate information about your Self. If you wait for days before journaling, there will be thousands of other thoughts that entered your mind and altered your original thoughts and reactions.

Eventually, you will understand the need to lose yourself in the journaling process: it is instrumental to the inward seeking process. Each participant finds her or his best way of delving into the expansive journey of discovering Self. And then inexplicably, other new discoveries begin to cross your path illuminating the 'More' with whom you coexist. You are not alone! We are not alone! There is so much 'More' than we ever imagined available.

Dear Readers, I think we, you and I, just discovered that *The Power of Thoughts* is more than just a Self-Help Book. Re-reading the Message from the Companions reminds me to open my heart and mind to EVERYONE from everywhere. So limited are we in our lack of curiosity to learn about others with whom we coexist.

What would it be like if we just accepted the idea of changing? WAIT!! Don't run away from the question. Please just entertain the possibility that change might improve your life, and you in turn might improve someone else's life.

What would it be like if we chose not to fear change? What if we accepted the reality that facing fear doesn't necessarily mean that we are going to lose something? What if we accepted that some things need to be left behind, while others just need a little bit of refinement? What if we trusted that we are capable of discerning what can be disposed of and what continues to remain? What if we trusted our fellow Readers to do the same?

In the previous chapter, we were introduced to the idea of the beauty of differences, and we were encouraged to think about the enormous amount of information that is available to us because of our individual perspectives. What if we chose to re-think our steadfast viewpoints? What if we considered delving into just a few of the differing perspectives that prevail among us?

For instance, instead of being instantaneously suspicious about someone whom we know nothing about, perhaps we might choose to be curious, open-hearted, welcoming and friendly. Just imagine what the world would be like if everyone chose that approach!

Dear Ones, there is much to be learned about the beautiful differences that exist among all the species that inhabit this planet and those that reside beyond. So, let's move forward with patience, kindness, and compassion for all that we encounter.

Chapter Seven

The Power of Thoughts is a handbook intended to awaken you to the distractive nature of your mind. Please do not shy away from this opportunity. Embrace it and rest assured that you are not the only person on the planet who has an impressively active mind that is constantly operating even when you are unaware of its activities.

Before this chapter began, the Companions gave me a pep talk, encouraging me to focus attentively so that the chapter could quickly be received and concluded. My attention span lasted through the first paragraph. Then I was compelled to brush my teeth, grab my wedding ring and earrings, and then of course, I had to check the ever so important emails. It's interesting to observe the tenacity of the mind's preferences. None of this needed to be done, but the mind preferred to do something other than focusing upon a book that encourages people to command their minds.

This small example is relevant for numerous reasons. **It demonstrates how easily the mind takes charge and how**

quickly we follow its whims. It also apprises us to observe how often these 'little' distractions happen throughout the day. Currently, my mind is thinking about extending the little distraction into a larger one. Let's get a cup of hot chocolate and quickly check on the garden as well. And then there are the bills to pay and the emails to return. You get the picture, Dear Friends.

We all have tasks that must be done, and some are more urgent than others, but it seems convenient that the mind comes up with these ideas in those moments when it would rather do something other than what I personally want/need to do. This begs one to wonder...**Who is in charge?**

For those of you who do not know me, I am a taskmaster. Admittedly, in my younger years my abilities were sharper and more efficient, but these skills still exist. It's fascinating to watch how much time is lost following the lead of a mind, who apparently believes it is in charge.

Observe your mind, Dear Readers! Hopefully, your mind has better manners than mine. However, you will not really know what your mind is up to unless you start paying attention to how it operates. For some of you this will be an easy task, while others will find it complicated. Pardon me for speaking the truth, but the mind is sneaky and very clever. If you really want to know who is in charge, then designate time to thoroughly observe and understand how your mind is functioning. Learn how it works with you and learn how it works without you.

Also, observe how much time you lose following its commands. This may be a real eye opener for some of you. It certainly was for me...and still is.

Please understand this discussion is about studying your mind so that it will be more efficient, more competent, and more cooperative as you move through your daily commitments.

Whether it is at work or play,
how does your mind serve you
and how does it limit you?

This is the information that you are seeking. This is why it is essential to learn everything you can about the workings of your mind.

The point of our efforts throughout this book is to present various ways in which You, the Reader, can learn how to examine your mind and how to confront it when it is necessary. Yes, there are times when the mind needs to be confronted. One way of envisioning this is to think of your mind as a child: you decide what age you want to assign to your mind. Initially this may seem confusing, but just pick an age and if you need to alter it later, do so.

Children, teenagers, young adults, as well as older folks often need to confront their behavior. It's a means of staying centered and focused on becoming the better person, the Beautiful You, that we are all intended to be. Confronting one's behavior means paying attention to your actions, observing the impact you have on Self and others, and making necessary adjustments that are needed to keep you on track.

These steps can also be used when observing your mind. **Pay attention to what your mind is doing, which means listen to the thoughts that race through your mind.** And jot them down! The need for notes will become evident when you engage with this journey of self-discovery. You may be surprised by what you discover, and hopefully, you will choose to accept the information with grace and kindness. **The goal is to gather information to improve the workings of your mind which will in turn improve your way of being in the world**. Accept what comes with intentions of self-improvement.

Your first exploration into observing your mind may be mind-blowing, but remember, you are in charge. Quickly accept that a commitment to this process will be wise. Allot ten minutes, twice a day, to investigate your mind's mannerisms. Consider it a time to visit the inner workings of the mind but avoid dwelling there. As you feel more accustomed to this exploration process, you will find the need to lengthen the amount of time you spend observing your mind's behavior and, along the way, you will discern the adjustments that need to be made. Dear Reader, please teach and treat the mind with the same tenderness and care that you do a child, and just like the child, the mind will mature, and evolve, and become a better servant to the world.

In the next chapter, we will delve more deeply into this process, but for now, please just be satisfied with the content of this chapter. Be kind to you. Be patient with you. Have compassion for you.

In peace be, Dear Reader.

Chapter Eight

*W*elcome, Dear Reader! Now is the moment to prepare yourself for an important adventure! Please focus upon the four suggestions below:

- Begin by choosing to accept this experience as an intentional action that you are pursuing for your personal well-being and your highest good.
- Congratulate yourself for having the courage to take this step that has the potential of changing your future.
- Envision the other Readers around the world who are also courageously participating in this act of goodness and send them waves of gratitude and appreciation.
- Take a deep breath and imagine what the world will be like, if individuals just like you choose to take charge of their minds.

Dear Readers, you have already joined the adventure. Having just read the preparation phase of our exploration process, now it is time to access your favorite device or your preferred journal and pen to record the thoughts of your mind. This will require some of your precious time, so you decide if this is the right time to pursue this adventure. Hopefully you will act now, but if it is not possible, then make a date with yourself. Please follow through with this exploration...**it's important!**

Step One

- Reread the first suggestion above.
- Then recall what your immediate thoughts were when you initially read the suggestion. Did you experience excitement? Did you respond negatively? Did your mind engage with the suggestion or breeze through it without giving it any thought?
- Please try to record each thought that raced through your mind. Include every detail that you can remember.
- Repeat this process with each suggestion.

Now that you have completed the first round of observing your mind, let's take a few deep breaths before we repeat the process. While you are settling down, please continue to notice what your mind is up to. When you are ready, proceed to the next step.

Step Two

- Reread the first suggestion again.
- Notice what your thoughts are doing now.
- Notice your reactions, feelings, attitude, demeanor, etc.

- Record every detail that you observe.
- Repeat this process with each suggestion.

Congratulations! You have completed your first intentional observation of the workings of your mind. Please spend time with the information that you gathered. Each time you think about this topic, you will find that the mind has many new ideas. It will have new opinions and new ways to manage the exploration process. And rest assured, it will also have new ways of avoiding the process. Such is life!

Everything you learn about your highly active mind will assist you in teaching it to be a remarkable assistant in your life. Essentially, what this means is YOU ARE IN CHARGE! Dear Reader, with this leadership role comes responsibility. Accept it with grace, dignity, and commitment.

Obviously, your mind needs much more attention. Just like a child that needs loving guidance, so too does your mind. Remember that raising a child takes time. Years later when they are grown and in charge of themselves, they still occasionally need attention from their parents. Likewise, your mind still requires much more attention for you to truly understand how it serves you and how it disrupts you. So, accept the reality that you have many more observations to make as you continue to educate your mind. Since your mind is an associate that will assist you in becoming the Beautiful Self you are intended to be, it is wise to foster a healthy relationship with this mind of yours.

Rest now, Dear Reader, before you proceed to the next chapter.

Chapter Nine

"**G**reetings, Dear Readers! We desire to be in your presence once again. As you gain more information about the functioning of your mind, we observe you with joy in our hearts. We yearn to be in communication with you as we were long ago. Although only a few remember the ease with which we once connected, the possibilities for the future excite us.

There was a time when Your Kind and Our Kind communicated frequently. We shared stories of the past and stories of that 'time.' We long to have these heartfelt interactions again.

Dear Old Friends, we are here! Even though you have forgotten our long-standing relationship, it still exists. We approach you now because you are in need of our assistance. We are always available to assist you, but over time Your Kind forgot about our presence. We approach you now because your circumstances are precarious. We desire to be of assistance.

As is obvious, the planet Earth is consistently experiencing unusual climate activity. This situation demands attention. More and more individuals around the planet are opening their hearts to this reality; however, the majority of the population remains in denial and continues to perpetrate harmful acts against the planet. Mother Earth does not deserve these blatant acts of cruelty, nor can she continue to bear this abuse.

Humankind must face the changes that are transpiring, and you must change your ways. Climate changes are directly related to misguided human actions. Dear Ones, this cannot continue. Many pragmatic actions must be taken on behalf of the planet. This is not a polite suggestion; it is pronouncement of necessity. Decisions among all nations must be made and collaboratively executed.

While these plans are devised and implemented, every individual on Mother Earth can personally participate in changing the ill will that you create and disperse around the planet. Let it be known that the toxic energy created by ill will is devastating to Earth's health. Every thought of unkindness, every meanness that is inflicted towards another, every act of harmful intentions that occurs upon the planet is witnessed and absorbed by Mother Earth. She cannot escape your ill will! Your misguided behaviors must be addressed immediately. And fortunately, it can be done!

Dear Old Friends, you are capable of changing your ways. Many of your misdeeds have become poor habits that repeat themselves without your notice. You have negative thoughts and do not even know they are happening because you are so accustomed to hearing the constant chattering that goes on in your mind. And when you are aware of your negative thoughts, you erroneously think and believe that they cause no harm. This is a misconception. Unspoken negative thoughts are as powerful and destructive as those that are spoken. Please do not delude yourself into thinking that you are righteous because you have not spoken meanness aloud.

Likewise, do not believe the misconception that the Earth is nothing more than a big rock that you can use, misuse, and abuse in any manner that suits you. Mother Earth is a Life Being that deserves the same respect as does every other Life Being that resides upon her. May we remind you that without Her generosity and hospitality, you would be homeless. Ponder this reality please, and then, perhaps you might realize that it is in your best interest to treat her with the utmost respect. While many who observe your species wonder why you are so heartless towards the Earth, others take notice of the lack of respect that you have for your own homeless species. Dear Friends, we speak bluntly, because you force us to do so.

The time is now! Please awaken to your selfish ways. You are a species with great potential and yet you squander your gifts and ignore those that you judge as less than you. This misbehavior cannot continue. Dear Old Friends, you are better than your present behaviors reveal. Please reclaim your humanity and become the Gracious People you are intended to be. Remember who you are! Remember who your neighbors are! Remember who Mother Earth is!

The differences you perceive are Gifts to be embraced. You all originated from the same Source. You are Brothers and Sisters blessed with the privilege of evolutionary choices. You are equal, you are same, you are Family. Embrace your diversity! Accept your differences with awe and respect. Remember, the Earthworm is as important to Existence as are you, and without its presence, Mother Earth would be less than she is now. Each of you is special, each of you has a purpose, each of you is needed, and each of you is loved and cherished equally by the Source from which you came.

Dear Children of the Earth, please remember who you really are and live your lives accordingly. Everyone, every Life Being you encounter is a member of your extended Family. Greet them with an open heart and with the same respect that you wish to be granted.

The Time is Now! Love Thy Neighbor!"

Chapter Ten

Again, we have encountered a visit from the Companions who make this book possible. Their message is challenging to read. You may have had some knee jerk reactions to some of the comments that were made. Please accept your immediate reactions as information that can be reviewed, examined, and expounded upon.

Once again, we have been provided with material from which we can study the actions of the mind. Open your heart to this method of observing your mind so that you can thoroughly understand the functioning of your mind including how and when it serves you and how and when it confuses you with distractions and/or disruptions.

Remember, Dear Friends, you are not alone in this process. Your mind is not the only mind on the planet that acts out. In fact, one of the advantages of participating in this process is that you come to realize you are not the only person who experiences frustrations with his or her mind. In truth this is one of the many ways that all members of the human species are alike regardless of gender, skin color, religious affiliations etc., etc., etc. You all have a mind that needs your attention. Accept this similarity as common ground from which conversation and connection can commence.

So, Dear Readers of *The Power of Thoughts*, let's use this recent message as a means for studying the idiosyncrasies of the mind. By now, you know the routine. We want to observe the mind in the moment as it is reacting to some type of stimulation. And yes, remember to keep a record of your experience for future reference.

Whenever you are ready to pursue this new adventure of self-exploration, please begin with:

Several long, deep breaths.
Allow yourself to relax.
Take more deep breaths as needed.
Gently, respectfully ask your mind to be quiet.
Accept what comes.
Take more deep breaths.

Dear Reader, continue to be led by your breath. Regardless of what unfolds as you observe your mind, consider it to be valuable information that will assist you in becoming the Beautiful Self that you already are. Rest assured you are already who you are intended to be even if your behavior is not as you wish it to be. Avail yourself of your breath throughout this exercise. Doing so will enable you to observe with clarity, to understand with compassion, and to accept with grace the changes that are yet to come.

Dear One, please return to the recently read message from the Companions.

- Read the first two paragraphs.
- Notice your mind's reactions.
- How do you feel about the invitation for communication and connection?
- Are your thoughts and your feelings in alignment?
- Record the details of your thoughts and your feelings.

When you are ready to proceed, please continue.

- Read the next three paragraphs (3,4, & 5).
- Observe your mind's reactions.
- Listen to your thoughts.
- Listen to any chatter that may be happening.
- How do you feel about the offer of assistance?
- How do you feel about the pronouncement of Earth's declining health?
- Review the mind's reactions again.
- Are your thoughts and your feelings in alignment?
- Record all details that are unfolding.

Take a brief rest if needed, and then proceed again.

- Read the next three paragraphs (6,7, & 8).
- Observe your mind's reactions.
- As you delve more deeply into the message, do you notice any changes in your mind's reactions?
- How is your mind reacting to the commentary regarding humankind's ill will?

- How do you feel about this commentary?
- How did your mind respond to the idea that it sometimes endlessly chatters?
- Do you recognize this habit within you?
- How do you feel about your discovery of this?
- How did your mind react to unspoken negative thoughts?
- How do you feel about learning this?
- How did your mind react to the mistreatment of the Earth?
- How do you feel about the bluntness of the message?
- Pause for a moment and simply be with your discoveries.
- Are your thoughts and your feelings in alignment?
- Record the details of your thoughts and your feelings.

If a brief rest is needed, please take care of yourself. Proceed again when ready.

- Read the remaining paragraphs (9-12).
- Carefully observe your mind's reactions.
- How did your mind react to the challenging commentary of the message?
- How do you feel about the challenges?
- How do you feel about the call to reclaim your humanity?
- Pause for a moment and contemplate this request.
- How did your mind react to the idea that our species should embrace and accept the differences within our species?

- How do you feel about this proposal?
- Are your thoughts and your feelings in alignment?
- Record the details of everything that you observed.

Dear Reader, thank you for participating in this exercise. Rest for a moment while you continue to feel the aftermath of this experience. This was not an easy task. Please congratulate yourself for facing the challenges of the Companion's message.

Recognize that your thoughts and your feelings are still in functioning mode. In essence, the exercise continues to have impact. Even though you have completed the tasks of the exercise, your mind continues to process what transpired. Take advantage of this situation to continue observing your remarkable mind at work.

Over and over again, you will have opportunities to learn more about the inner workings of the mind that are a crucial part of your human experience. The thoughts you think influence your behavior even when you are unaware that it is happening. Hopefully, through these exercises, you are gaining greater awareness of how your mind assists you and how it undermines your preferences. Having this knowledge improves your ability to align your thoughts, your feelings, and your intentions.

Dear Reader, by opening your heart to self-exploration, you are becoming the person you truly want to be and are intended to be. Like all your fellow human beings, you are a work in process. By developing a greater relationship with your mind, you truly are more in command of your life.

Rest Dear Friend. In peace be.

Chapter Eleven

*"**B**eloved Children of the Earth, we come with gratitude in our hearts. For so long we have attempted to gain the attention of the human species. Dear Friends, you are needed! We reach out to you through **The Power of Thoughts** in hopes that you may respond to our plea for help.*

We understand that our presence may be a surprise to you. As said before, we mean no harm. Our hope is that you will give us the opportunity to prove our intentions. We come on behalf of the Planet Earth. As you well know, she is the home for countless species, including yours. She has been a vibrant member of the Existential Family, and she is revered by all others in Existence.

Currently, the state of her health is alarming. It is for this reason that we seek your assistance. As you may remember in our earlier message, we seek your permission to be of assistance. Without your permission, we cannot assist you; therefore, we ask again for your permission to assist you. The blatant truth is this: you need our assistance to survive this global catastrophe, and we need your assistance to orchestrate the recovery process.

There are many factors involved in restoring the Earth's health. We applaud those who currently implement plans to improve the environment. Cleansing the oceanic waters is essential to the future and must be continued. Ending the misuse of her bodily fluids for powering human homes, automobiles, and factories is another critical issue that needs immediate attention. And stripping the planet of her forests and her grass lands are also actions that must be stopped immediately. These pragmatic down-to-Earth issues can no longer be ignored or delayed. Resolutions must be made, and actions must be taken now.

People from all walks of life will play a role in this act of mercy. Those who actually participate in correcting these practical and critically urgent issues will be a small percentage of the Earth's population, while a much larger part of the population will play another extremely important role by addressing the issues of ill will that plague the planet.

The task is large. When one encounters such an expansive disruption in the core beliefs of a civilization, one is initially paralyzed by the enormity of the situation. So much must change, and yet, one does not know where to begin. The sense of despair is overwhelming and leaves one in a state of hopelessness. The people of Earth are currently locked in a reality of misconception. Indeed the situation is grim, but it is not impenetrable.

Dear Ones, you are a species who thrives upon expansion, facing one challenge after another throughout your evolutionary experience. This is another challenge that must be addressed individually and globally. The old-world view of division and separateness can no longer be acceptable. Your species has outgrown this way of being, but the transition continues to be resisted. In essence, there is a strain of resistance that avoids maturation. This collective continues to believe in a concept that never was true. They embrace the misunderstanding that some are better than others. This erroneous thinking fuels the ill will that sickens your species.

Another misunderstanding that compromises your evolutionary process is the belief that this strain of resistance is incapable of change. Please challenge this misunderstanding. Just because someone believes something is true does not mean that it is. The majority of your species has evolved beyond this way of thinking. The masses believe that you are all Brothers and Sisters and they are grasping the reality that your differences are an asset that increases the species' potential.

Those who fear losing their presumed power may struggle with this concept and not realize that they are the weak link in your evolutionary development. Although they remain problematic, they are capable of change.

Change is the element of growth that must be sought. Many of Your Kind want to help the Earth's health issues, but do not know where to begin or how to proceed. They are the masses of your population who can make a profound difference in assisting the Earth by facing the ill will that exists within each of them.

Be not afraid! Be not ashamed! Fear and shame will not assist the cause. In truth, they will worsen the situation. Dear

Claudia Helt

Friends, simply accept that you are in need of improvement. Ill will is a plague that requires no medication. It is an illness that demands attention, observation, acceptance, perseverance, and willingness to change.

Forgive our bluntness, but humans are a species that quickly and easily see the flaws in others, but they struggle with noticing and accepting their own flaws. This is your challenge! Empower yourselves, Dear Friends, by accepting the reality that you need to reclaim your humanity. It is time to review, refine, and renew your skills that enable you to Love Thy Neighbor.

Ponder this, Dear Friend. You are more than you appear to be. Seek the inner You and rid the Earth of ill will by doing so."

Chapter Twelve

*D*ear Readers, take a deep breath. Before probing into this next chapter, let's breathe together with all the other Readers around the planet, who also just finished reading the third message from the Companions. As was said, we are all Sisters and Brothers sharing a common issue that demands our attention.

We were told that we suffer from a condition that is so pervasive and destructive that it is of plague proportions, and we were informed that our condition referred to as our ill will is the primary factor in Mother Earth's declining health. This is an uncomfortable message to read. Understandably, none of us wishes to believe that we are a person of ill will. Can this be true? Can humankind's ill will truly be so bad that it warrants being described as a plague?

Dear Reader, please take another deep breath. Take several if needed. For many of us, the most recent message challenges our sense of Self. Let's face it, no one wants to believe that they are a carrier of any negativity, much less ill will. Nor do we want to believe that our own spoken and unspoken thoughts are harming the Earth. This suggestion begs one to wonder what percentage of the population ever imagined that this was a possibility. Perhaps it is time to put our imagination to work.

Let's give this topic the attention that was suggested. Let's face this challenge together so that each of us can personally determine whether he or she is a person of ill will.

With another deep breath, let us proceed with this new exploration of Self. Let's begin our journey remembering that we are not alone. Envision your Brothers and Sisters who are also reading *The Power of Thoughts,* standing with you and creating the positive energy that is necessary to continue this journey. We must begin by releasing previous ideas that we have regarding the definition of ill will. Particularly in this moment many of us are thinking that people of ill will are the worst of the worst. They are murderers, vicious criminals, violent perpetrators, sex traffickers, child abusers, and more and more. Indeed, these worst of the worst are definitely part of the issue. Their toxic energy poisons the planet and everyone else that reads, watches, or listens to the news reports regarding their horrible deeds. It's easy for us recognize ill will in such violent acts of cruelty. And it's also easy for us to say, I'm not one of "those" people. I am not like that, and I am not a person of ill will.

Anyone who has been a victim of ill will or a witness to ill will can attest to the terrible, long-lasting impact of such inhumane behavior. To elaborate by using a fictitious example, the negative impact of an act of ill will would be similar to this scenario:

- The act occurs,
- the victim in undescribed ways is tragically harmed or worse,
- the Earth witnesses and feels the impact of these ruthless act of unkindness,
- conjointly, others who witnessed the event are as impacted as was the Earth,
- then the wave of ill will affects everyone who is in the victim's primary circle of connection,
- and then the news media provides reports of the act of ill will extending its impact to unknown numbers.

As you can see, such an incident can have far more toxic influence than one can imagine. Essentially, not only the victim, but family members, friends, co-workers, countless unknown individuals, and Mother Earth all experience an encounter with ill will. The Earth was mentioned last to honor the loved ones of the victim. However, please make a note for future contemplation. Mother Earth was featured in this fictitious example because she is present when each act of ill will unfolds. She experiences every act of ill will that occurs upon her. Ponder this Dear Reader, when you have a moment to do so.

So many incidents of human ill will transpire daily that they have unfortunately become commonplace. To survive the reality of our loss of humanity, many of us have developed ways of deflecting the assault of information by quickly setting it aside so that we can avoid feeling the repercussions of the events. One might assume that this is a good way of handling the situation, but this is an erroneous assumption. Ill will exists, and pretending that it doesn't accomplishes nothing except allowing it to continue to spread.

Regrettably, many if not most humans live without truly being cognizant of the negative impact that this toxic energy imposes upon us. Liken it to an asymptomatic disease. The individual is ill, but unaware that he or she is inflicted.

Dear Readers, now that we have a vision of the extremely toxic energy created by the worst of the worst, let us address the toxic energy that the rest of us create on a daily basis. Yes, Dear Ones, we too create and carry ill will, and yes, most of us are unaware of the damage that it causes.

Our next step into Self exploration will be an opportunity to awaken to the human flaws that we possess, which may or may not be known to us. Once again, we are advised not to be afraid. Dear Ones, even if there are parts of you that you do not wish to reveal, BE NOT AFRAID! The inner work that you are pursuing is between you and yourself. Rest assured you are not the only person who has flaws. Consider your flaws to be the steppingstones of your evolutionary development. Embrace this opportunity to discover more about your Self in the privacy of your own home.

Exploring the ill will that exists within is a worthy and essential act of kindness that will assist humankind in reclaiming their humanity. Not only will each of us benefit from the excursion, but everyone we encounter will also benefit from our improved nature.

By learning more about the operational style of our own ill will, we will once again be in command of our lives. Rather than living in oblivion, pretending that everything is right with the world, we can choose to seek more information about our personal ill will and learn the truth about what is really happening within and around us. With this new knowledge, each of us truly can eliminate ill will from our thoughts and our behavioral system. This determined act of kindness can significantly improve Earth's health. By removing our personal toxicity, the energy associated with our ill will, the Earth will essentially have breathing room again, which will give her time and space to heal while the pragmatic measures necessary for sustainability are being completed on her behalf.

Dear Readers, gaining knowledge about the impact of our own ill will is an act of good will that we must all embrace. Frankly, researching the ill will of humankind and making the necessary changes to eliminate it places each of us in a position of becoming a humanitarian. Selflessly participating in this act of kindness can change the energy of the planet and bring peace to the Earth. Everyone, including the Earth, will benefit from our efforts.

As you well know by now, we are about to embark upon another exploration of Self. Prepare for another deep dive. Once again, these exercises will demand attention, so please discern when it is best for you to address your issues of ill will.

We begin with a deep breath. Dear Readers, have you noticed the repeated messages presented throughout these chapters inviting you to take a deep breath? Hopefully, you are learning to appreciate the importance of this simple act that is absolutely necessary for everyone, including Mother Earth. She is a Life Being that has needs not unlike our own. We must breathe to live. So must She!

As we slowly awaken to the issues of our poor stewardship of the planet, Mother Earth's rivers, oceans, lands, and sky continue to be sickened by the toxic waste dumped into her once beautiful connective systems. Yes, this is still happening even though the signs of her distress are obvious. While more complaints and knowledge come forward about the pollution that humans have created, Mother Earth continues to bear the consequences of our selfish decisions. This cannot continue. We cannot allow this to continue.

Facing our ill will is the first step that must be taken. Accepting that altruistic changes must be made is the next step. The third step is implementing, maintaining, and sustaining the changes that have been made. Our willingness to participate in this necessary act of goodness will assist Mother Earth's recovery. She needs time and space to breathe freely again. As we take our deep breaths to engage with our ill will, She will have opportunities to take deep breaths as well and while we face our ill will, She will share our sorrows, just as She has always done. Mother Earth will be with us, and as our ill will diminishes, her strength and health will improve, and She will faithfully witness our evolutionary development knowing that we and all the other species that reside upon her will benefit from our efforts of kindness and good will.

So, as we take our deep breaths for the journey ahead, know that Mother Earth is inhaling and exhaling with us. Continue your breath work until you are ready to begin your new adventure of Self-discovery.

Dear Readers, please open your hearts to the reality that ill will is part of your life. You experience it from others, and it also wells up from within. The extent to which you are personally accountable remains for you to discover. Embarking upon this research is truly a personal self-study project. This is not about discovering who has the most ill will or who has the least. We are not here to point fingers at who is the best or the worst. That type of discussion would most likely result in an increased level of ill will around the globe. Obviously, that is not the desired goal.

Let's remember that the goal is to discover and carefully study the ill will that inflicts us. What we learn will not make us better than another or worse than another. However, our discoveries hopefully will help us understand how we are afflicted by the ill will of others, while also educating us as to how we afflict ourselves and others with our own personally generated ill will.

Because it is easier for most of us to detect the flaws in someone else rather than in ourselves, it is best if we begin our process by first learning about the ill will of others. As you prepare yourself for observing the ill will syndrome in another person, please make a quick note to Self.

Dear Self,

It is very likely that someone else is presently observing and studying my own ill will! Yikes! Be on best behavior!

Exude Kindness,
Self

This humorous gentle reminder hopefully will assist each of us in monitoring our observations so that we avoid the ill-fated inclination of judging others. This is easier said than done; nevertheless, we must challenge ourselves as we explore this very serious and ubiquitous human habit. As we consciously pursue ill will, our newly found awareness of its presence may be shocking. Because of this, everyone is encouraged to proceed slowly, carefully, openheartedly, and compassionately.

Remember this is an exploration process about our human nature. We are here to gather information from other individuals who will not be aware that they are being observed. Just as we are confused about our own ill will habits, so too would they be if they were aware of this human tendency. Point being, we must approach this project with kindness and tenderheartedness as our guide. Hopefully, in the very near future there will be heartfelt conversations about this potentially life-altering topic, but at this point, we are just gathering information.

Our best approach to this Self-exploration project is to envision our Brothers and Sisters around the globe who are also taking this important step. Wish them well with their exploratory experiences and send them positive energy from your heart to their hearts. Urge everyone to proceed with love and kindness and thank them for the efforts that they are making for the sake of humankind. As we enter this next phase of evolutionary development, let us also express gratitude to all those individuals, friends, family, neighbors, strangers, etc. that we will be observing. Because of them, we will gain greater understanding about our own flaws and together we will make the necessary changes to rejuvenate Mother Earth and in so doing become the better people we are intended to be. Remembering that we are all One, we take the next step.

Exercise for Observing the Habits of Ill Will

Preparation:

Open your heart, Dear Readers, to consciously witnessing examples of ill will that unfold around you. Whether it happens in your home, on the bus, at the grocery store, on your early morning walk, at your place of work, or wherever it may be, please be alert to the moment. Ill will appears in many different forms, and often we do not even recognize it. The day will come when we look back and say, "How did I miss that?"

Fortunately, the steps that we are taking will change our perspectives. Soon we will recognize the subtle presence of ill will as easily and quickly as we do currently

77

when it is so powerfully present that we cannot possibly misunderstand what is happening. This is why ill will needs to be studied. Much can be learned if we pay attention to what is unfolding before us, around us, and within us. By increasing our awareness of ill will and educating ourselves to its habitual antics, we will learn ways to manage it and hopefully eliminate it from our species.

In preparing for our observational experiences, each of us would be wise to create a personal commitment to self-care. Some suggestions have been listed below. Please access these if they feel right for you or feel free to create your own list.

Commitment To Self-Care

- Accepting the reality that these observations may be unpleasant at times, I make a commitment to take care of myself.
- I will set boundaries regarding the length of time that I will expend observing each day.
- I will not allow observations to interfere with my normal schedule.
- When I notice a moment of ill will, I will capture the situation as best I can and then continue with my day. I will jot down notes if possible.
- If my conscious awareness of ill will reaches a state of overload, I will stop my observations and focus my attention elsewhere. I understand that I am not

expected or intended to endure the discomfort of observing ill will.

- If a toxic moment is too taxing, I will remove myself from the situation.
- I will refer to these statements of self-care regularly and add others as is needed.

Our next step in preparing ourselves for exploring the various aspects of ill will is to anticipate how this may happen, where and when it may unfold, and who may be the one who teaches us about ill will. Although it is impossible to orchestrate exactly what might transpire, we can imagine how it might play out. For instance, there is always opportunity for ill will to spread when people rise in the morning. A family member gets up on the wrong side of the bed and a clashing of minds occurs. Sparks of ill will flare, as the participants shake their heads and wonder what went wrong. Much can be learned from such an event.

Each individual in such an imaginary situation has a perspective that will enhance our knowledge about the developmental process of an act of ill will. For instance, one family member can be the initiator of ill will, and another can be the recipient. Let's also imagine another family member that plays the role as a witness of the event, while a fourth member of the family takes on the role of being befuddled by the entire experience and wonders how it ever happened. Obviously in real life, this type of scenario can range from being very subtle to being outrageously hostile with long lasting impact. Whatever the level of this imaginary disruption might have been, it is an opportunity to learn a great deal about ill will.

In this situation, we have four participants who were immediately affected by the event. Let's pretend for comfort's sake that this was a low-level disruption. The scenario begins with one member of the family (the initiator) waking out of sorts. We have no other information about this individual other than he or she caused the upset. The negative energy emitted by this family member affected the rest of the family whether they were consciously aware of the impact or not.

By using this imaginary scenario, let's attempt to gather some information about what transpired.

- Did this person even know that his or her mood created negative energy?
- Did this person know that the negative energy generated within him or her afflicted the entire family?
- Did this person know that he or she was spreading ill will?

The next family member (the recipient) felt the first wave of the initiator's negative energy.

- Did the recipient know why the initiator was out of sorts?
- Did the recipient know that the initiator's mood generated negative energy from within which then spread to others?
- Did the recipient understand that this negative energy was ill will that had afflicted the entire family?

The next family member (the witness) observed what transpired and was equally afflicted by the ill will that was dispersed to the entire family.

- Did this individual know why the disruption had occurred?
- Did this individual understand that this incident transpired because the initiator took his or her disgruntlement out inappropriately?
- Did this individual know that there was another way of expressing one's emotions?
- Did this individual understand that he or she was afflicted by the ill will generated by the initiator?

The remaining family member (the befuddled one) who was at a loss by what happened was still equally afflicted by the situation.

- Did this family member have any idea that the family incident was the site of a negative energy disruption that affected every member in the family?
- Did this family member have any awareness that he or she was afflicted with the ill will that was instantaneously generated by one of the family members in the early morning hour?

As you can see, this disruption, like many other disruptions, happens in a moment and then spills over to those who are in close proximity. However, these incidents rarely are confined within the incident location.

As many of you know, even the smallest disruption that occurs in your home typically expands outside of the home. The victims of the incident, regardless of its level of intensity, carries the ill will outside into the community. The aftermath can take on various symptoms. One of the family members, seeking guidance, may share what happened with a confidant, and then that listener is afflicted by the negative energy. Another family member may brood about the situation for hours, not knowing that the negative energy that he or she is generating internally is spreading to those nearby. The possibilities of spreading ill will are similar to those of a contagious disease. One individual, not knowing that he or she is sick, can spread the disease to countless others on the bus, at work, in school, walking down the street, at the market, on a plane, etc. It happens! So too is the impact of ill will. It exists! It has impact! And it spreads!

Hopefully, you grasp the simplicity of ill will's expansion, and also, the complexity of recognizing and solving the problem.

Dear Readers, the more we learn about the ill will that exists within us and around us, the better equipped we will be to manage this global issue. As with most complicated issues, we must look within first. How can we possibly think that we can erase ill will from the world if we do not understand the ill will within us.

As you navigated this chapter, perhaps you identified with some of the examples that were provided, or maybe the examples nudged you to remember some of your own experiences. While reading about ill will can be educative and helpful, it pales to actually remembering and addressing a personal event. Whatever experience you had during this chapter, please applaud yourself. It takes courage to face challenges, particularly when the challenge entails reviewing one's personal flaws.

Dear Readers, appreciate what you have done, and appreciate what your Brothers and Sisters have also done. This was a chapter that demanded a great deal of time and attention. Whatever your actions and reactions were, you deserve praise. And even if you had to close the book and stop your process, still feel good about yourself.

Learning about ill will is not fun, but it is necessary. We can change the energy of the Earth by ridding ourselves of negative energy. The more we learn about it, the less impact it will have upon us, and eventually we will consciously choose to avoid generating negative energy. It can be done. We can gain command of our lives, we can reclaim our humanity, and we can bring peace to the Earth.

Dear Friends, this is a statement to be remembered, a thought to be repeated, and a commitment to be fulfilled.

We can bring peace to the Earth!

Chapter Thirteen

*D*ear Reader, please take a deep breath and envision yourself in your most favorite place. Be still in this preferred place that brings you great pleasure and simply enjoy the beauty of the moment. Rest in your favorite space as you prepare yourself for another reading experience. Know that you are not alone on this journey of Self-discovery. Accept the presence of your unknown Brothers and Sisters who also are resting in their favorite places. Accept their good wishes and send good wishes to these yet to be known Friends. Breathe in, knowing they are doing the same. Breath out, merging with the breaths of these new Friends. Allow the union of positive energy being generated by each participant to nourish the hearts and souls of Everyone present.

Embrace the moment.
Cherish the moment.
Reside in the moment.

In gratitude, let us begin this new chapter with open hearts and deep-felt connections.

"Greetings, Dear Readers! So grateful are we to be in your presence. We join with you now for heartfelt reasons. The time is now! Many of you are accustomed to hearing or reading this small message that has been repeated throughout the ages. For some, it has become so prevalent that it has unfortunately lost its powerful impact. For others, it may be the first time to encounter this timely and profoundly important communication. To all who are presently reading **The Power of Thoughts,** *please clear your mind of other thoughts. The message of old remains as important now as when it was first articulated.* **The Time is Now!**

Dear Readers, thank you for your attention. Our intention is not to frighten you, but to assist you. We come with news that must be considered. Although we do not wish to be bearers of unfortunate news, we must speak the truth, for your future depends upon it. Throughout this book, you have been alerted to the reality of the ill will that consumes the people of the planet Earth. It is uncomfortable to accept such information. No one wishes to believe that they are a carrier of such an unfortunate illness. No one wishes to be the victim of such unpleasantness, and yet, one must accept the reality of one's circumstances. Dear Friends, please do not fall victim to your own fears.

There is reason for hope. *We are here because this situation can be altered. This is a curable disease. If we were not certain of this, we would not be here attempting* *to assist you. Your situation demands attention now! We speak boldly because it is necessary. No longer can you ignore your circumstances. The time is now!*

Several steps must be taken, and each of you must participate in this healing process. You cannot designate someone else to do this for you. Dear Ones, each of you:

- *must accept the reality that ill will exists within you, and you*
- *must accept responsibility for eliminating this dreadful negative energy that generates from within.*

By accepting these two steps, *you empower yourself and others to advance forward. As said before, there is reason for hope. Once the problem is recognized for what it is, you, the peoples of Earth, can eliminate this unhealthy ill will from your systems and alter the course of the future.*

Please have no shame about this unwanted disease. It simply is. When it developed and how is not relevant. There is no one to blame, no one to point fingers at. What is, is and what must transpire depends upon each of you. Everyone must accept the burden of cleansing this destructive illness from his or her own being. This can be done!"

There is reason for hope!

Dear Readers, we have received another message that awakens us to reality and calls us to task. Shall we broach the task now by clearing our minds of other thoughts and by focusing our attention upon the intention of the message?

Just clearing one's thoughts is a task in itself...a most worthy task that opens new doors to new pathways that can alter one's current ways of existing.

So, begin your clearing process by welcoming in numerous deep breaths. You know the routine. Just do what is best for you and move into the state of silence where your thoughts are dim or non-existent and where your heart is open to whatever comes through.

When you reach a sense of calmness and openheartedness, please decide to address the message just read. Making the decision to proceed is an act of free will. **By doing so, you pronounce your willingness to participate in the noble efforts of eliminating ill will from yourself and from the planet Earth.**

Ponder this last statement, Dear Reader, and observe your reactions and thoughts.

- Has your mood changed?
- Do you feel yourself being pulled away from the quiet state that you just created?
- If so, choose to quiet your thoughts again and regain your composure by re-focusing your attention to calmness and openheartedness.

This is a wonderful moment for you to embrace your efforts. Whether you momentarily lost your composure or if you are still maintaining it, praise yourself for recognizing whatever is happening. In either situation, you are in the present, which is where you need to be.

The truth is...the statement which inferred that you were pronouncing your commitment to eliminate ill will was boldly presented for a reason.

|t made the reality real!

You were no longer just thinking about the possibility of addressing ill will, you were freely considering participating in the "noble efforts" of eliminating it from yourself and Mother Earth. This was a rapid transition! One moment you were meandering about in a state of calmness, and then you were on the brink of a very important decision. It makes sense, Dear Reader, that you might be taken aback by the rapid series of changes.

So again, please praise your efforts and accept that there is more going on here that demands your attention.

"Indeed, much more is transpiring that requires your utmost attention. You are in transition, Dear Friends! Breathe that truth in and allow yourself to accept what has just been read. You are in transition, and you are responsible for this advancement. Praise yourself, Dear Readers!

As you gain more knowledge about the workings of your mind, you truly will be in command of your mind and your life. *Being aware of your mind's activities means that you have control over the ill will that generates within. You* *will be consciously aware of everything the mind is doing. With that information, you can diminish and eliminate the negative energy, the ill will, from your system.*

*Dear Readers, this is not a ruse. It is reality! Paying attention to the workings of your mind frees you from being controlled by the mind. Many of you will find it hard to believe that you have been undermined by your mind. It is unbelievable! And it is also true. The good people of Earth are good people. And yet, these good people have been and continue to be brewers of ill will. This unbelievable situation is true, and it can be corrected. **There is reason for hope!***

*No longer do you need to live in unawareness. Simply observe the antics of your mind and you will learn that your mind has been misleading you for a very long time. That time is over. Now, it is time to live in awareness, which was always intended. Dear Readers, you are but an observation away from being in command of your life, now in the present, and in your future. **Imagine this, Dear Reader, and as you do, accept the truth of this reality.***"

The messages received never cease to amaze me. No matter how baffling a message initially seems to be, the clarity of the communique eventually unveils itself. Sometimes, the revelation comes quickly. Sometimes, it does not. The latter demands patience and willingness to pursue the true meaning of any given message. And there are times, Dear Readers, when the pursuit requires courage.

Over the many years of receiving these messages, I have come to accept that every message is presented for a reason. Indeed, our current message brings forward extremely unpleasant news that demands our attention. It is not a message that anyone in their right mind would want to engage with; however, the message speaks the truth and we, each of us, must give this message the credence that it deserves.

The message does not judge humankind as 'bad people.' It does not blame anyone for our unfortunate circumstances. Instead, the message boldly speaks the truth of our situation and reassures us that there is reason for hope. We are the victims of our own ill will, and we are the solution to this unthinkable problem.

Our ill will can be changed into good will! As was said in the message, we have the power to correct this problem. Once we accept the reality that we are indeed carriers of ill will, then and only then can we move forward in eradicating ill will from our species.

Dear Readers, we are more than we appear to be. We are remarkable people now, even as we struggle with our ill will. Imagine what we will be like, and what our world will be like when we release all the ill will that now burdens us and replace it with the Good Will that we are intended to share with our Brothers and Sisters.

Ponder this, Dear Friends! Accept the reality of our present circumstances and imagine who we will be when we are free of our ill will.

There is reason for hope!
We are the reason there is hope!

Chapter Fourteen

*O*pen your hearts, Dear Readers, to the opportunity, the privilege, of participating in a significant role in the elimination of ill will from the planet Earth. In so doing, you will cleanse your own body of this toxic negative energy while assisting others to do the same. As ill will diminishes, Mother Earth's declining health will reset. With the alleviation of humankind's ill will, this Blessed Life Being, the planet that we call Home, will be able to recover from our tragic misuse of her resources.

Hopefully, we humans will finally grasp what our ill will has done. Because of our blatant disregard for the Earth's needs, we have created a catastrophic potentiality. The reality of this potent possibility is not misinformation. Evidence of this truth is available throughout all nations. Those who attempt to discredit this information are not in alignment with the needs of the Earth. Unfortunately, these individuals continue to place their shortsighted preferences above all others, which will without doubt lead our future into an unthinkable disaster.

Dear Readers, the time is now! Those of us who do care about the future can choose to create another path. The power of good will far outweighs the negative, misguided energy of ill will. We have forgotten this. We have become so accustomed to living in this uncomfortable state that we forgot who we really are.

If saving the Earth means that we need to improve ourselves, then let's do it. Let's ignite our current level of good well to a more expansive and intentional level that will focus upon rescuing the Earth. Now that we are aware that our thoughts and our habits create negative energy, let's do something about this. Let's change our ways.

I personally do not like the idea that I am a person of ill will. It's shocking! And I do not want to continue this way of being. While I prefer to think of myself as a good person, clearly, it is time for me to review my behavior and my thoughts to be sure that what I think is the truth. I anticipate finding things about myself that will be disappointing, but that's okay. I'm eager and willing to make necessary changes so that I am really interacting with others from a perspective of good will.

We can do this, Dear Readers! Just as we did the previous exercises throughout this book, we can do this important exercise together as well. Let's face our ill will together. Life is always about change. This is just another opportunity to make changes that are in our best interest, which will actually have an important impact not only on ourselves, but also everyone around us, including Mother Earth.

So, Dear Readers, Dear Friends, remember your yet to be known Friends across the planet with whom you did all the previous exercises. Envision them again in your mind and calm yourself by breathing in and breathing out with all your Brothers and Sisters around the world.

Breathing in, we recognize the importance of this exercise. Breathing out, we share our positive energy with one another. What a lovely gesture! We connect with one another through this easy yet powerful encounter. Envisioning each other and welcoming this exchange allows us to expand our good will with one another. Who knew that this could be so easy?

Just think about this, Dear Friends. Those of us who might have doubts about making changes may want to give this another thought. We are all grounded in good will. We came into being innately as carriers of good will. And we have experiences receiving and giving the goodness that exists throughout our society.

Unfortunately, it is true that many of us also have experienced the aftermath of ill will. It doesn't take too many acts of ill will to make one super vigilant and self-protective. We have memories when our own ill will reacted in ways that we regret, even those reactions that were necessary self-protection in the moment. There are memories that will demand more attention than others, and fortunately, we have better ways to heal those old painful experiences.

We have more information now, Dear Friends. We are aware of the power of our thoughts, and we know that we have the power to command our thoughts. No longer are we victims of our own thoughts.

We are a remarkable resilient species. With this new awareness about the workings of our mind, we can make positive choices to improve our way of being. This is a wonderful opportunity to improve ourselves. And the reality that we can work in union with others who have the same desires for self-improvement is exciting and inspirational. We can do this! Let's do the right thing for Mother Earth, for our Friends and Families, and for Ourselves!

So, as we move into this new phase of expansion, let us once again envision the other Readers who are doing the same. Remember they are wonderful people, who desire to improve their selves, just as we do. Remember they have similar doubts and fears, just as we do, and remember that everyone involved in this transformative action means well. This is all about rejuvenating the good will within us. There will be times when we need support, and there will be times when we will offer support to others. Envision this process! People all over the planet, different ages, different ethnicities, different colors, different genders, different languages...different, yet the same...all wanting to improve humankind. What Grace this is! The Children of God working together to save Mother Earth.

Part Two

Saving the Earth by Improving Your Mind

Chapter One

*T*he sun is rising! The alarm that always successfully awakens me does not originate from a bedside clock. It comes from my mind. How this happens is beyond my scope of knowledge, but the bottom line is this. It works!

The sunrise is my favorite time of the day...the quiet hour that allows for so much more than just the beautiful view provided by Divine artistry. Indeed, the view itself is a compelling justification for getting out of bed and racing to the oceanside where the horizon's newest painting will rapidly unfold before my eyes in mere minutes. Photos will be frantically taken, tears will fall, and long deep breaths will follow.

What joy the sunrise brings! Even on those days when the sun is hidden by cloudy skies, you know something awesome is happening beyond the clouds. I confess that my preference is a spectacular array of colors, but the cloudy days, even the rainy days hold great allure as well.

And what does one do after the sun has risen and the Divine Performance is over?

Hmm! Well, that's a question for the ages. Truly, this is a question that has great potential. Each of you who is reading this story will have your own unique answers to this question. Just imagine sitting around with your circle of friends and posing this question. Go ahead! Envision how your friends might respond. How would you respond?

Perhaps, Dear Reader, you are wondering why this is happening. Previously, you were engaged with a self-help book, and now the format has changed, and you seem to be involved with a story about someone who is nuts about sunrises.

In truth, you are involved with a fictional story that will hopefully illustrate the intentions of the self-help book. The characters of this story are based upon people just like you, Dear Reader, as well as the Brothers and Sisters that were envisioned throughout the self-help book. These characters were created to be role models for us as we shift from our old ways of being into our new way of being. Through these fictional characters we will witness our goodness and our ill will. Together we will face our flaws, accept that they are real, and release them as quickly as possible.

Each of us has a history filled with many experiences of all kinds. We must honor and cherish the good times and the good will that we've encountered, and we must also face those experiences that still burden us. To improve ourselves, we must embrace the positive activities of our past and we must also release the negative experiences so that they no longer weigh us down. It is time to put the negative stories of our past to rest.

Now that we understand that our thoughts have a huge factor in our wellness, we can choose to carefully review the negative incidents that we've had. If there are issues that can immediately be tossed aside, do so with gratitude and recognition of the role that they have played in your life.

Those situations that are more complex may require several reviews to conclude their power over your current life. Do not fear this, Dear Friend. You have already survived whatever traumas you incurred, and you will also survive the process of reviewing the old experiences.

By learning how to command our thoughts, these old repetitive memories can finally come to an end. Meanwhile, we will have successfully improved ourselves and awakened our good will to take a prominent role in our lives again.

So, Dear Readers, let's continue our story by returning to the provocative question that was described both as a question for the ages and as a question that had great potential.

"Michael, I had an interesting experience during sunrise this morning. It gave me pause." Sandy stopped rushing about the kitchen and faced her husband who was also rushing about. "But," she said shaking her head and throwing her hands in the air, "You know how life is, particularly in the morning. One doesn't have time to pause. At least I don't!" she declared. "Anyway, as the sunrise was concluding its debut, I heard a voice coming from somewhere that asked, 'And what does one do after the sun has risen and the Divine Performance is over?'

"What do you think that means, Michael?" Sandy stared at her husband as he stared back at her. "Am I supposed to make a To Do List for everything I need to address today? That doesn't seem right to me, since I do that daily anyway."

Sandy's tone of voice changed taking on a more serious tenor. "The question seems bigger than that, Michael. Actually, it seems to be profoundly important. I don't why I am feeling this way, but I do, and I don't have a clue as to what I am supposed to do about this."

"Well," Michael quietly replied. "This experience has definitely piqued your curiosity. Typically, when that happens, it means you are on the brink of a learning opportunity. So maybe you should take a few quick notes before your workday begins. That usually helps you in these situations." Michael's comments quickly calmed Sandy. She walked him to the door expressing her appreciation for his suggestions, and then enjoyed a big hug before he left for work. Sandy knew Michael was right. She did need to take a few notes for later when she would have time to give this situation the attention it deserved. Whatever was happening would be revealed at just the right time in just the perfect place.

Michael and Sandy Anderson became best friends the first day that they met in Mrs. Sargent's otherworldly classroom. At age 6, these two very quiet children were assigned seats, side by side. The wise teacher's first assignment for her new class was to invite the children to introduce themselves to the person sitting next to them. Little did Michael and Sandy know then where this assignment would take them. As advised, the children faced each other, and then skipped over the introduction by asking in unison, "Can you believe this room?"

Curiosity superseded their shyness as each child scanned the room. Fingers pointed to one oddity in the classroom to another while many whispers and giggles were exchanged before the two children finally introduced themselves. During that brief encounter, Sandy and Michael sized each other up. The friendship was bonded.

The couple often reminisce about Mrs. Sargent. Even though she has long passed, they continue to thank her for bringing them together.

Sandy's busy morning continued to be busy as she quickly scribbled a few notes about her sunrise experience, which then led to the quickest shower ever taken in history. One would wonder if it was even worth the time, but it readied her for the preparations that were necessary to face the workday. Of course, the all-important To Do List, which she was deeply attached to, had to be completed. Sandy believed and was absolutely convinced that the workday could not begin without it. Just as the last item was added to the list, the phone rang. At first, she was annoyed until she saw her Dear Friend's name pop up on the phone.

"Jennifer!" she declared excitedly. "How are you? Tell me everything but do it quickly!" Jennifer, responding with equal enthusiasm, was also in a rush.

"All is well," she said rapidly, "but I do need some time to catch up. I need some 'SANDY TIME!'" which was their way of letting the other know that a conversation was necessary.

"I'm in the same place. I need JENNIFER TIME. Are you available for lunch?"

"YES!" replied her friend. "Same as always?"

"Yes, see you there!" answered Sandy.

Chapter Two

"**J**ennifer! Gosh, it is so good to see you! It seems like forever since we've had quality time together."

"I feel the same way! Even though it's only been a week!" The two friends laughed, acknowledging that 'stuff' always interfered with their needs to discuss everything that was going on in each other's life.

The waitress approached with a smile on her face. She was carrying two glasses of water, once with ice, and one without. Anyone watching would know that she was familiar with these customers. "You two again! Are you having the usual or are you going to live dangerously this week?" Greetings were exchanged as always, and then the 'usual' order was taken. The two friends have frequented this little café for years. And the waitress, who they have become very fond of, is one of the reasons they enjoy dining there. She made the place feel like home. This was their favorite hangout, where life's issues were revealed, discussed, and sometimes resolved. Tears were shared and great laughter was enjoyed in this sweet little café.

"So, what's going on with you?" asked Sandy as she struggled to get her jacket off. Jennifer leaned over to help with the resistant sleeve and then burst into tears.

"Oh, my goodness, Jen! What is going on?" Unable to respond, Jennifer reached for a Kleenex from her pocket and tried to subdue her emotions. Shaking her head, she finally managed to apologize for her behavior.

"No need for apologies, Friend. We've both been in this place before. Just take your time and the words will come when they are ready." Sandy laid her hand on Jennifer's and the magic of touch immediately calmed her tears. Several deep breaths were taken and then Jennifer was able to speak.

"Goodness!" she said. "We've only been here a few minutes and the waterworks are already unleashed. Do you have this impact on everyone, Sandy, or am I the only friend that acts like Niagara Falls?"

"We both have our moments, Dear Friend, and we are very fortunate to have one another. I am so, so grateful for our friendship."

"Me too!" whispered Jennifer.

"Your phone call was not a surprise this morning. I was in a whirlwind of emotions. Michael and I had a quick conversation about 'my stuff' before he went to work, and then, I immediately returned to my whirlwind. I was delighted when your call came through. We are both so lucky to have husbands who are loving and communicative, but let's face it, we need women friends. It's essential! As we both know, Dear Friend, our getting together today was no coincidence. So, take a deep breath and tell me everything."

Jennifer did as she was told. She closed her eyes and took a long deep breath and then several more. Eventually her eyes opened to find Sandy calmly sitting with her eyes closed as well. She waited a moment enjoying her Friend's sense of serenity.

"Serenity!" Sandy's eyes popped opened. "You should have seen me this morning!"

"You rascal! How do you do that?" demanded Jennifer. Sandy's blank face was evidence that she was clueless about what had just happened.

"Sandy, my Dear Gifted Friend, your skills are acting out again. You just responded to my thoughts!" Sandy's face turned red with embarrassment. Jennifer quickly abated the situation by returning the magic touch treatment. It worked!

"Geez! Exactly what did I do?"

Jennifer apprised her Friend of what had just happened, knowing full well that Sandy was unaware of the circumstances.

"Are you sure, Jen? I was certain that you made a comment about my sense of serenity?"

"Nope! But I was thinking about it. And you immediately responded to my thoughts." Jennifer's voice was gentle and firm. "You are amazing, Girl!"

"Amazing or crazy? Yikes! Enough about this topic!" Sandy shook her head as if she was desperately trying to rid herself of the experience. "Let's get back to you, Jennifer. What's going on that's causing the waterfall of tears?"

Jennifer fell silent and Sandy remained still holding the space for the words to come forward. As close as these two friends were, as safe as they felt with one another, it was still difficult to speak the first sentence. Finally, a loud sigh broke the silence. Jennifer thanked her friend for sitting quietly and patiently with her while she tried to sort through the thoughts that were racing through her head.

"There's so much I want to talk about, but trying to articulate my feelings is easier said than done." Sandy smiled, nodding her head in that particular way that infers mutual understanding. A look of relief crossed Jennifer's face. Sandy quietly engaged in a long deep breath that, without a spoken word, invited her Friend to do the same. And Jennifer responded in like manner.

"You really are a marvel, my Friend. Somehow you are able to gently nudge people like me in the right direction without even whispering a word." Closing her eyes again, Jennifer settled herself with a few more elongated breaths.

"Sandy, I think I'm lost!" The words spoken so softly and so sincerely brought tears to the surface again. Gentle tears…the kind that allow for healing to occur while the tiny droplets reverently carry the pain away. Once again, Sandy remained silent. She knew her Friend was perfectly capable of handling this situation, she just needed time, space, and a good companion nearby. It was a role that each had played for the other for a very long time.

"Whew! Thank goodness for our friendship! I'm already feeling better and the conversation hasn't even begun yet." Jennifer's laughter welcomed company and Sandy immediately joined in. This was a scene often repeated by these two characters. Healing began before the difficult discussion took place. The traditional high-five was shared celebrating the miracle of their friendship, just as Hazel, the angelic waitress approached with their lunch.

"Whoa! You two have already reached the high-five stage! This is good!" Everyone giggled again. "Well, get some nourishment before you get into the really big issues."

"Geez!" declared Sandy. "You really do have us nailed, Hazel! Thank you, Dear, this is perfect timing."

"My pleasure, ladies! Take good care of each other." As the waitress walked away, the 'ladies' stared at their bulging plates.

"Thank you, God! Thank you, God! Thank you, God!" prayed Jennifer.

"Amen!" added Sandy. The first bites were taken, the crunch was loudly audible, and rapture crossed their faces. "Oh my God! Mexican food is the greatest! Jen, thank you for loving tacos as much as I do. I knew we were going to be 'best friends' the minute you expressed your love for nachos and enchiladas! Thank God that our paths crossed." Laughter drifted through the dining area and applause was offered by Hazel and the other hard-working folks who made the café the special place that it was. Another delicious bite was taken before the conversation began.

"Okay," announced Jennifer. "I can talk about 'my issues' now!" As she spoke these words a thought about the medicinal benefits of Mexican food instantaneously raced through her mind. The thought tickled her, but she made no mention of it.

"So, this is the deal, Sandy. Something has been off for quite a while. I've known something was wrong, but I haven't been able to figure it out. Needless to say,

I am confused. I've tried ignoring it, but we both know that doesn't accomplish anything, and it just allows the confusion to shift into agitation.

"The truth is…well, I don't know if this is a truth or not, but it seems like…" Jennifer paused again. "It seems like I'm lonely…or that I'm missing something. This doesn't make any sense! You know that Tony and I are doing great. Everything is good and our lives are filled with wonderful, positive people and happenings. And still there is something missing, and Sandy, it feels like my heart is longing for something." Leaning back into her chair, Jennifer seemed to deflate.

"Okay! I've got the picture and we're going to talk through this, but first, you need to eat some more. You're exhausted from releasing all that worriment." Pushing Jen's dinner plate closer to the edge of the table, Sandy softly but firmly advised her to enjoy another taco. "And have some water, Dear. I think you may be dehydrated."

For a few minutes, the friends just focused on their lunch as if nothing had happened, but Sandy was carefully taking peeks to see that her Friend was okay. When it felt appropriate, she took the lead. "Congratulations, Girl!" The comment surprised Jennifer. "You've been doing some good work and at the same time carrying a big load." Jennifer responded by rolling her beautiful eyes.

"Hey You! Don't dismiss me. I'm being serious here!" They both giggled at Sandy's attempt at being firm and serious. She pretended to be miffed, but Jen knew she was just messing with her.

"Your support is definitely appreciated, Dear Friend, but I just don't seem to be making any progress." Once again, the magic of touch was necessary. Just a gentle laying of one hand over the other improved the energy around the table.

"This is big, Jen. And it's important. I really meant it when I said that you are doing good work. You are! And I would be so happy if you could accept that as a truth. Appreciate what you have done, including the fruitless attempt at ignoring whatever was going on. You quickly learned that path was not helpful. That effort was simply part of your gathering information phase.

"And...your ability to assess the goodness that surrounds you and Tony was really good work. Sometimes people get very confused and erroneously start blaming things on a family member or someone else in their circle, but that's not happening here. You have clarity about your family and social life. Your awareness of the goodness in your life is awesome." As the conversation continued, Jennifer seemed to brighten up. She was taking Sandy's complimentary comments to heart.

"Thank you, Dear Friend. Your support means the world to me."

"Well, that's what friends do for one another," stated Sandy nonchalantly. "But I have more to say. Can you continue with this conversation for a bit longer."

"Yes, absolutely, but can we have just a few more bites of our lunch first?" And this they did. Numerous yummy noises were made as the friends recharged from the delicious Mexican meal.

"I could eat this every day," Jennifer admitted. "Do you think we would get tired of Mexican food if we actually ate it every day?"

"Never!" asserted Sandy as she carefully placed her cutlery down on the plate. "So, are you ready to continue our conversation?" Jennifer nodded as she pushed her plate aside. Once again, the thought about the medicinal benefits of Mexican food raced through her mind.

"You crack me up!" quipped Sandy. "Of course, Mexican food is medicinal! Everybody knows that! Why do you think everybody eats it? It's health food, for goodness' sake!"

Jennifer burst into laughter. "You just did it again, Sandy! You're responding to my thoughts!"

"Well, I had to!" she said all-knowingly. "This is the second time you brought the subject up. And I just wanted to set the record straight. Mexican food is medicinal." Jen continued to giggle as Sandy promised her that she would try very hard not to intrude upon her thoughts again. And then she acknowledged, "I actually don't even know how this is happening, but I will attempt to learn more about this unusual so-called Gift of mine. Now, let's get back on task.

"You mentioned earlier that you felt like your heart was longing for something. Can we talk about that?" Jennifer's eyes immediately teared up. Sandy's intuition had led her to the tender point.

"Oh my." Jennifer's softly spoken words were barely audible. Instinct alerted Sandy to be quiet and patient while her Friend collected herself.

"Something is happening, Sandy, and I don't understand what it is. This just doesn't make sense. My life is wonderful. I am so blest. You know I'm speaking the truth. I'm not just making this up." Sandy nodded her head in agreement.

"And yet," Jennifer continued, "something is missing! I'm ashamed to say this, but there must be something more." Tears started to flow. Sandy wanted to ease her Friend's discomfort, but realized any comments at this point would disrupt Jenn's process.

"How can I be so selfish, Sandy? I have a wonderful life…and I want more! It is so embarrassing to talk about this. I feel like a whining spoiled brat.

"And yet, my heart aches for something that is beyond my comprehension. I am yearning for something, and I have no idea what it is." Jennifer paused. A large deep breath followed, tears were wiped from the cheeks, and the closing statement was announced. "That's my story, and I'm sticking to it!"

The two Friends sat quietly for a moment, each overwhelmed by her own personal emotions and also what seemed like thousands of thoughts. Jennifer felt relief from sharing her story and was embarrassed by having done so. Her worriment about her situation continued but for the moment was gratefully subdued. Sandy was filled with admiration for Jennifer's courage to share her concerns and extremely happy for the transition that she was undergoing. Her inclination was to believe that Jennifer was on the verge of discovering her true self and she was delighted for her.

"Hey, Dear Friend, are you ready to continue?" Sandy's question was so gentle that Jennifer could not refuse the invitation.

"You are such a good Friend, Sandy. How on Earth do you put up with me?"

"The same way you put up with me!" Sandy's smile warmed Jennifer's heart. She wondered why she was so fortunate to have such a good Friend.

"I'm going to sidestep that thought you just had, because I want to tell you how grateful I am to be part of this process. Your courage astounds me, Jen. I am so, so proud of you. And I am very excited for you."

"Excited for me!" Jennifer was completely surprised. "I'm very grateful for your kind words, but I don't understand. Why are you proud of me? And what courage are you referring to? Sandy, when I said that I felt lost, I really meant it. I don't know what's going on. And I have no idea how to work my way through this situation."

"YET!" inserted Sandy.

"Yet?" responded Jennifer.

"Yes, yet," agreed her Friend. "Dear One, let me try to explain myself. I'm sorry that my intentions were clumsy. I'm proud of you Jen, because of your willingness to face this unknown upheaval in your life. This is not easy. As you said before, it is confusing. Yet, even while carrying this burdensome confusion, you still attempted to address this unknown as best you could. That takes courage!

"When you mentioned that your heart was yearning for more, it reminded me of similar stories I have heard or read about. And that's why I am so excited for you! Usually when someone starts experiencing what you've described, it means that the person is in a phase of transition. It can be unsettling at first, but usually it means the individual is having a spiritual experience of some kind. Jen, this is a wonderful opportunity.

"You're doing what others have done throughout the ages when they were challenged by an unusual situation that seemed to be calling to them. The call seems compelling, yet no directions appear to be given that would provide a means of connecting with the unknown caller. But the call continues to create confusion for the individual who desperately desires to understand what the caller desires. Does this ring true with you, Jennifer?"

"Geez, Sandy, this gives me a lot to think about. As happy as I am with my wonderful life, there seems to be something missing. I just keep thinking and feeling that there must be more to life than what I am experiencing now. I just know, even though I don't know how I know it, that there is something more that I'm intended to do. Oh, Wow! I'm not a spoiled selfish brat after all. This really is important!"

"Yes, it really is, Jen! This is a very big deal!"

"Well, what am I supposed to do, Sandy? How do I manage this? Is there some book I should be reading? Oh, my goodness! This is so exciting, but I don't know how to do this."

"Okay, the first thing we do is take some deep breaths." The Dear Friends adjusted themselves in their dining chairs and did as was suggested. As is usual the case with deep breathing, they both began to relax.

"You're very good with deep breathing, Jen, and I suspect in the upcoming weeks you will become even more skillful with this calming process. Let's just quiet ourselves for a while and enjoy the discovery that you have made. What's happening to you is real. Even though it seemed odd and upsetting initially, it's actually a very wonderful opportunity. And it will unfold as it is intended to do." The brief moments of relaxation were very helpful. Jennifer was smiling from ear to ear and appeared to be at peace with what had occurred.

"Thank you, Sandy. This feels right! I am so grateful for your guidance and assistance. I'm afraid there will be many more conversations like this one in our future. I know that I will be turning to you for more support and guidance."

"Wonderful!" declared Sandy. "I can hardly wait. You know, Jennifer, the only thing that has changed since we started this conversation is your attitude. The situation itself has not changed, but your perception of it has. Before, you regarded the situation from a negative perspective, and you were diminishing yourself as if you had done something wrong. Now you are perceiving it as a positive opportunity with yet to be known possibilities. It's a profound shift. And it is so delightful to bear witness to the growth that is already happening. Thank you for letting me part of this exceptional moment."

"Sandy, your encouragement is very reassuring." Jennifer paused for a moment. Many, many thoughts raced about in her head. She was very excited and maybe a little bit scared about what she was getting into. But the excitement was definitely overriding the fear. She wondered if she was on a journey and then realized she had no idea what a journey was. Then she pondered if she should get a journal for this unusual opportunity/experience/journey? *"Geez,"* she said internally, *I don't even know what to call this adventure. I just wish there was a magical book out in the Universe that could give me a jump start on this exploration."*

"Jen there are many books available that you will find beneficial. I'm not sure that they are magical, but they are definitely filled with wisdom." Sandy smiled at her Friend. Both were acutely aware that she once again was responding to Jennifer's thoughts.

"However," continued Sandy. "I want to share a tidbit of wisdom with you that I learned from a very wise woman. She urged me to focus on the experience itself rather than searching for answers from books. She also knew me very well and accepted the reality that I would be going to the bookstore regardless of her guidance. So, she strongly advised me to buy only one book at a time. Her exact words were:

'Dear One, you know how books consume you! As alluring as books are, do not distract yourself from the experience that is unfolding before you. Manage how much you read a day. And allot your other free time to writing about your experiences. Whether you are up on down emotionally, write about it! Your notes facilitate your growth, while the books validate what you are doing and have done. Find a nice balance that aligns with your exploration process.'"

"Well, that was precious information! Do you have any other tidbits to share with me?" Jennifer's energy was back. Her excitement was visibly noticeable.

"Actually, I do, Jen. I'm reading a book now about the power of thoughts and I think you will find some of the information very relevant with what you are currently going through. I bought the book, as you might imagine, to find out what's going on with me and these weird experiences that I've been having. It's fascinating, but we can talk about that at another time.

"One of the tidbits that I would like to share with you is the author's invitation to welcome all the challenges that unfold during your inward journey, which is the term she uses for such experiences. She urges the Reader to embrace each new encounter equally with an open heart and a curious mind and she fully believes that the exploration phase will be much more pleasant if the participant proceeds with patience and compassion while leaving self-criticism and negativity behind.

"In regard to self-care, the author suggests that anyone who chooses to follow the path of the inward journey should consider developing a practice that praises one's efforts. She states no matter how large or small an action is; the participant should applaud him or herself and appreciate the effort that was made and the information that was gained. Isn't this a lovely way to approach any new project? Praising your steps taken while expressing gratitude for the knowledge gained."

Sandy fell silent, trying to remember if there were any other suggestions that she could share with her Friend. Jennifer, recognizing what her Friend was doing, leaned over and placed her hand over Sandy's. The magic touch accomplished its task.

"Thank You! I do not know how you can carry so much wisdom in that heart of yours. Dear Friend, you have just provided me with everything anyone needs to start a new adventure. My gratitude has reached the point of being inexpressible." Jennifer took a moment for a deep breath and managed to find a few more words to share.

"My Dear Friend, Sandy, you have renewed my energy. You have inspired courage within me. And you have given me bountiful, unconditional Love. I am so, so grateful."

With that said, Hazel, the angelic waitress, appeared from out of nowhere. "You two do remarkable work," she said as she cleaned the table. Then she pulled the check our of her pocket and placed it in the middle of the table. "So very blest you are to have this friendship. Keep taking good care of each other. I'll hold you in my prayers during the week." And off she went.

As did the two Dear Friends. Hugs and more words of gratitude were exchanged outside of the café before each went in her own direction.

Chapter Three

"*What* does one do after the sun has risen and the Divine Performance is over?"

The question posed by some unknown voice during Sandy's early morning walk continued to visit her throughout the day. "What does this mean?" she asked the empty room. Sitting at her writing table didn't seem to facilitate any writing, so Sandy opted for ten minutes of Yoga stretches. Hoping the gentle exercises would clear her head of the repeated question regarding the sunrise, she noticed her mind shifting to another engaging topic. Sandy's day was so busy that she had no time to process her time with Jennifer. Each time a thought about their conversation attempted to insert itself, a smile crossed her face, but the mind quickly move onto another task and the moment was lost.

As she focused on stretches for her back, she allowed her mind to replay some of their conversations. She giggled about their ridiculous, but truthful, comments about Mexican food and wished she hadn't devoured the entire plate of food. *"Geez!"* She scolded herself. *"Why didn't you save at least one taco for a snack?"*

The simple thought of having a delicious taco made her want to race out and get a To-Go-Dinner. "Good Grief, Sandy! You are an addict! Get a grip. There's food in the fridge and there is no need to distract yourself with visions of Mexican food."

Sandy's mind declined her logic and attempted to persuade her to place an order for the taco deluxe dinner. Fortunately, she was aware of the mind's antics. "Nope!" She announced loudly. "We are not going to order Mexican food!"

As she continued her back stretches, Sandy marveled at the tenacity of her mind.

"Even when I am aware that my mind is taking me places that I do not want to go, it is extremely difficult to override my mind's preferences. How did this come about?" she thought to herself. *"Sometimes I feel like I'm battling with another consciousness within me. Sandy is inside of me doing what she needs and prefers to do, and then, this other entity comes along and believes that it is in charge. This is so weird!"*

"Ugh, enough!" she spoke aloud. "Focus on your neck stretches, Girl." And this she did. Sandy discovered Yoga years ago when she had joined a meditation class in hopes that she would find a way to manage her anxiety. The class was very helpful, and Yoga became a lifestyle. Both relaxation methods focus upon the breath, which for her was and is the means to serenity, command of self, and resilience.

As she flexed her neck and shoulder muscles, a smile came to her face. Another memory from her time with Jennifer rushed through her beautiful mind. *"Welcome every challenge with an open heart and a curious mind."*

"Yes!" she said gleefully. "That's what I need to be doing with this mysterious question! I need to turn on my curious mind and open my heart to this morning's question rather than tiptoeing around it."

Sandy's excitement shifted her desires. The Yoga had relaxed her, facilitating a new approach to the question that seemed to be reaching out to her. Rather than viewing it from a suspicious perspective, she was now able to open her heart to exploring the question from a curious viewpoint. Then, as if summoned, another thought popped into her mind. It was no coincidence. It was a reminder of Michael's suggestion before he departed for work. He urged her to take some quick notes about the experience.

"Of course, I took notes!" She leaped across the room, grabbed her journal and rapidly turned the pages to the most recent entry. "Ah!" she sighed. After reading her notes several times, Sandy grabbed her journal and relocated to a favorite chair with a view of the backyard. The birdfeeder was like a busy airport with flights arriving from all directions. Birds of all types were sharing their evening meal with one another. *"Look at all the diversity,"* she thought. *"They don't seem to have any issues about differences. Our species could learn a lot from these beautiful creatures. They seem to have a much greater awareness of mutual co-existence than do we."* Watching the birds added another level of calmness to Sandy's demeanor. Her breathing shifted as she enjoyed the company of the backyard friends. Even though her eyes were still open, she was in a meditative state.

The question she had heard in the early morning hour returned as a whisper. *"What does one do after the sun has risen and the Divine Performance is over?"* Sandy welcomed the question and invited the Whisperer to sit in the chair across from her. "Enjoy the view, Dear Friend." Sandy continued her quiet moment as if a Dear Old Friend were meditating with her. It was a lovely experience. The angst she had felt most of the day about the mysterious question was gone. She was still curious and eager to understand the message within the question, but she was no longer worried about it. Her perspective had changed, and the fitful mind had stopped projecting unwarranted negative thoughts about the question's intentions.

Sandy took a long deep breath and envisioned her visitor doing the same. She opened the journal which was sitting in her lap and quietly turned the pages to the last entry. All her movements were very quiet because she did not want to disturb her unseen companion. With her favorite pen in hand, she began to reflect upon the question.

"Dear Journal, as you know I am here to gain understanding about the mysterious question that was heard this morning on my walk. I'm convinced there is a message within this question. Similar to my Friend Jennifer, I feel as if this unknown message is calling to me, and for reasons that I cannot explain, this feels important. I know my mind can sometimes take me in the wrong direction, but I don't feel that is happening. This weird experience seems

real to me, and I think there is a reason for whatever is happening. I do not believe this is a coincidence.

As you are acutely aware, Dear Journal of mine, the book that I am currently reading encourages the Readers to welcome all challenges with an open heart and a curious mind. I shared this with Jennifer at lunch and it profoundly shifted her mood and perspective. And while Jen and I discussed the information from the book, it had a similar effect on me. By envisioning the Whisperer of the question, I am following the guidance of the author who frequently encouraged the Reader to imagine the other Readers who were sharing the same reading experience. In so doing, a sense of camaraderie developed within the Reader. In my own way, I have essentially created a sense of connection with the Whisperer and hopefully a bond will develop between us. Oh, Dear Journal, hope burns eternal.

Ah! Another thought comes to mind about Jennifer's description of her heart aching for something. That image rings true for me. I've been so busy of late that I don't seem to have time for anything but one task after another. Sitting here, as I am now, is so delightful. I feel like me! There is more to life than the busyness. Somehow, I must regain my balance. I'm out of alignment. I'm not in touch with myself because I am too busy being elsewhere. I've lost connection with my inner Self and with my wonderful spiritual journey that brings joy and expansion to my life. Oh, my goodness! This is the message within the question!"

Sandy looked up from her journal and stared at the empty chair across from her. "Thank you, Whisperer! The message is received!" Tears welled up in her eyes as she felt the warmth of an unseen embrace. "Don't worry about me. I can change this around. I just needed a little nudge. Thank you for getting me back on track."

As the warmth of the embrace faded away, Sandy still felt the aftermath. She gazed at the empty chair and wondered. *"Are you there or is it just my imagination?"* Viewing the situation from a curious nature made her smile. *"I don't need an answer to that question,"* she whispered to the empty chair, *"but maybe, someday, you might wish to give me a sign."* And then the most delightful thing happened. A lovely little Song Sparrow flew up to window, stared at the empty chair, and then filled the silence with her wonderful aria. A coincidence? Doubtful!

Chapter Four

"*W*elcome home, Stranger! You've had a very long day!" The couple exchanged a kiss while Michael continued to free himself from his coat, the briefcase, and a beautiful bouquet of flowers.

"For you, Dear One! Sorry, I'm late again!" Michael's work was taking a toll. He was as busy, if not busier than Sandy, but fortunately, she rarely had to work overtime.

Walking towards the kitchen, Sandy expressed her gratitude for the flowers and reassured Michael that they were not needed. "The flowers are always appreciated, Dear, but this lovely gesture is not necessary. It just adds another task to your day. How is the project progressing?"

Typically, Michael didn't like to discuss work at home. Once he walked out of the office, he didn't want to think about it anymore. But this evening was different. "Sandy, I don't know how to motivate the team. They're dragging their feet. And this isn't like them! They are good people. Dedicated and highly motivated, but this project has become an unpleasant burden! I feel stuck. The team feels stuck. It's a mess!" His frustration was obvious, but more importantly his concern about his team and the project was stressful and exhausting.

"Oh, Mike, I'm so sorry," she accentuated her sincere words with a big hug. "Tell me how I can help. Do you want to talk first or eat first?"

"Both!" he replied.

"Great! Just go sit down," she said pointing to the table. "Or would you prefer the living room? We're having chili. That's easy to eat in the comfy chairs." Michael immediately turned and headed for his favorite chair. This was not like him. Normally, he would insist upon helping in the kitchen. Tonight, he had no energy to do so. "Perfect choice! Everything is ready. I'll join you with haste." In minutes, the meal was served and the beautiful flowers, nicely arranged, were sitting on the coffee table.

"You're a magician! How did you manage this so quickly?" Her wonderfully kind and spent husband stared at his bowl of chili and then took a long deep breath. Sandy wondered if he was too tired to eat. "Oh, no!" he responded to her thought. "I'm just preparing myself for the first bite of your awesome chili. Shall we take the first bite together?" This was a long-standing ritual that began in the early days of their courting. It was an opportunity for each of them to be exceptionally present to the other. The first bite was a significant moment of togetherness that was cherished and celebrated. "Thank you, Sandy. This is exactly what I need."

"I thought you might need some medicinal food, and as we both know, with the assistance of Mexican food all concerns can be resolved."

"You are a woman of wisdom, Sandy. I'm already feeling better."

"Good! Then let's talk about this issue at work, if you like." Sandy's invitation was quickly accepted.

Michael's style of dealing with issues usually involved the solo approach. Seldom did he want to discuss anything with someone else until he had already solved the problem. On the rare occasions that he did want to discuss an issue, Sandy was the person he trusted to have such a conversation. "I don't know what to do!" His comment came across with a greater volume than was usual, which was another indicator of how rattled he was about the project.

Sandy sighed loudly and followed it with several deep breaths in hope that her husband would follow her lead. It worked. "Thanks for the role modeling, Dear Wife of mine. You're right, of course, I do need to breathe into this situation. Our present approach simply isn't working. The efforts made, which have been many, have resulted with only minimal progress and I think we have lost our confidence. In truth, I think we've reached the point of fear." Michael slumped back into his chair, closed his eyes, and focused on his breath. *"I cannot let this get the best of me. There must be a way to break this cycle of fear that is strangling our creativity."*

Sandy's unusual, yet ordinary skill allowed her to hear Michael's unspoken words. These incidents of telepathy were so frequently experienced between the couple that they had grown accustomed to them. She waited a moment before responding, not wanting to interrupt his thought process.

"It's okay, Dear, you are not interrupting. I would love to hear your feedback. Your energy shifted so I suspect you have an idea to share with me." Anyone who witnessed this exchange might be a bit confused, but for these two, it was just their normal way of communicating.

"Well, your thoughts really touched me, Michael. I think your answer lies within your comment. Your team, at this point, is focusing upon the wrong issue. As you said, 'You cannot let this get the best of you.' That's exactly what is going on. The fear component is strangling you and your team of your creativity. So, the goal at this point is to face the fear, which we both know is not an easy thing to do. And it's particularly difficult, when you're not aware that the fear exists. That's the task, Michael. First, address your fear, and then assist your team in addressing their fears. It will be an extremely beneficial experience for all of them. Address the fear, Michael. And the creativity and the confidence will return."

"Geez, Sandy! You're amazing!" Her husband's energy was rejuvenated. He was a completely different person than the one who had walked through the door less than an hour before. He was Michael, again. "And you make it sound so easy, Sandy. Can it really be an easy experience to accomplish?" She thought about the question before quickly spouting out an answer.

"The answer to your question is 'Hopefully!' We both know that facing one's fear varies from one person to the next, and each individual has his or her hurdles to jump, but what do you have to lose? Currently your team is lost. As you said, the project is an unpleasant burden. The energy of your team must shift their perspective. They no longer look forward to coming to work because the project has become a huge negative factor in their lives. Can you imagine the thoughts that are going through their minds? They must be drowning in their own negativity."

Michael sat silently as Sandy's voice replayed in his head. *"She's nailed it."* Sandy's husband said from within. *"Everything she said rings true."*

"Sweetheart, I need help. I cannot expect my team to change their perspective, until I change my own."

Sandy nodded her head in agreement but remained silent so that her sweetheart could work his way out of this abyss. "Abyss," he whispered. "That certainly describes my view of the situation. This past week our attitudes have gone from bad to worse, and I haven't been able to see an escape from this deep abyss that we've been in. So, how do I rescue my team from this unacceptable place?" Michael's mind returned to its old ways, immediately trying to sort everything out. His anxiety shot up and the stress overwhelmed him again.

"Whoa! Hold on Michael! You're jumping the gun!" Sandy's intervention quickly stopped Michael from diving into the abyss again. "Remember, you need a new approach. This one isn't working for you anymore. It may be useful again in some other situation, but for now, you need an approach that will serve you, which will then help you to help your team.

"It's interesting that your situation brings to mind the same book that Jennifer and I discussed at lunch today. It's a self-help book that focuses upon the power of thoughts.

And needless to say, you and your team have been having lots of thoughts about this project. The author stresses the importance of being aware of our thoughts. While some, hopefully most, of our thoughts are beneficial to us, others are not. I suspect that a large number of the thoughts racing about in your head regarding the project are not serving you well. Same for the team.

"An important suggestion made by the author has to do with the curious mind. She believes that having a greater understanding of your curious mind will enhance all aspects of your life. And she encourages her Readers to explore their curious mind via deep breathing exercises. That should work for you, Michael. You enjoy doing breathwork." Michael's curiosity was definitely piqued. He wanted to know more and urged Sandy to continue.

"Well, she begins by inviting the Readers to participate in a five-minute exercise. Then she guides them to take several deep breaths and follows with three simple instructions. 1) Listen to your Breath. 2) Listen to the Silence. 3) Simply be in the Silence. After the five minutes is up, she asks the Readers to review their thoughts when they were invited to be in the Silence. And then she urges the Readers to discern if their thoughts served them well or if they were an impediment. Then she asked how they might improve their thought processes.

"The point being is that the author is teaching the Reader how to become more aware of the influence of their thoughts." Sandy took a deep breath. She apologized for her off-the-cuff summation of the book. "Michael, you might like to read the book for yourself. It's so much more expansive than I just shared with you. But I hope you got a sense of how it may help you with your momentary paralysis with this project.

The author also shared a profound statement that really touched me at the time...and still does. *You are in command of your life. The mind is not your leader, you are its leader!*

"Isn't that a powerful statement? We need to remember that one, Michael. Let's face it! We cannot believe everything we think, so we need to be on top of this. It's in our best interest to know what our thoughts are impressing upon us."

Michael's mind was in gear cogitating what his Dear Love had just shared with him. Fortunately, he was in charge and aware of all the thoughts that were rapidly generating ideas, asking questions, pondering different options, etc. "The mind is an incredible asset when it's working with us," he mused, "but it seems that the mind is not always a good team player. Hmm. I'm recognizing that my mind is a conundrum that requires much more of my attention.

"Sandy, I am interested in reading the book. I think it will help me and the team to resolve our problems. It's just been heartbreaking to see them in this unbearable slump. They are such good people. Curious, creative people who love their work and love to do their best. They don't deserve this." He paused for a moment and then a hopeful and confident expression crossed his face. "A group retreat is in our future!"

Michael's transformation from the person who arrived home a while ago to the person who was now relaxing in his comfy chair was mind-blowing. He looked years younger.

Sandy wished she had taken Before and After photos to substantiate the difference.

"Sounds to me that I am looking like my youthful, handsome self!" Michael's response to Sandy's unspoken wishes provoked a round of giggles between the couple.

"How does this happen, Mike? You know we're weird, don't you?"

"Speak for yourself, Dear!" laughed Mike.

"Well, how many couples do you know who can hear each other's thoughts? Better yet, how many people do you know who can communicate in this way." The room fell silent. Michael stared into nothingness as Sandy waited for an answer.

"Not enough, Dear," he said softly. "But someday, there will be more."

"So, you acknowledge that you know other people who have this ability?" Sandy's curiosity immediately lit up. She so wanted to meet other people who share this unusual ability. Having Jennifer in her life was a godsend. She didn't have to monitor herself when she was in her company. Actually, Jennifer was as curious about what she referred to as the "phenomenon" as was Sandy.

"I acknowledge, Dear One, that like you, I long to have more people in our lives who also have this Gift. We are not the only ones that possess this skillset, Sandy, but at times, it feels that way. This is another conundrum in our lives that demands more of our attention. At this point, we just take this incredible ability for granted. That in itself is amazing, and what is even more unbelievable is that we are not able to share this Gift with others. We can't even talk about it except to one another, because we don't want people to think we are weird."

Again, the room went silent. Each was pondering the situation and wondering what their options were.

"I wonder what would happen if we just came out about this to our dearest friends." Sandy gave her husband a moment to reflect upon this before she continued. "You know Jennifer already knows about it. She catches me responding to her thoughts on a regular basis and she doesn't think that it's weird. She thinks it is fascinating and she wants to learn more about it."

"Do you think this self-help book that you're reading could help us strategize a plan for doing this?" Michael's interest inspired Sandy.

"I think it may, Dear, and it so pleases me that you are open to this idea." She leaned forward in her chair and grinned at her Beloved. "I love you so much!"

In return, he leaned forward and said, "I love you more!"

And in unison, they said, "Tomorrow is another day!"

Chapter Five

"*What does one do after the sun has risen and the Divine Performance is over?*" As the Andersons prepared for bed, the question that consumed Sandy's attention a few days beford popped into her mind again. Her immediate response was, *"Not now, please! I need a good night's sleep!"*

"What's going on, Sandy? I thought you were tired."

"Sorry to disturb you, Mike. That sunrise question just came to mind. I'll try to keep my thoughts to myself." They both giggled about that and then rolled over in opposite directions as if that might solve the problem. Sandy tried very hard to stop the chatter in her head, but worried that she might still be interrupting Michael. Knowing that he was the one who really need a good rest she decided to visit her Sacred Space. She had no plans to engage in anything but distraction until she entered the room and saw the Journal sitting on her chair. She didn't remember leaving it there, but there it was, nevertheless.

Sandy sat down, wrapped herself in a warm shawl, and flipped through the pages looking for the last entry. She read the last paragraph from her previous writings. "Oh, goodness," she sighed. "How did I stray so far away from my inward journey? When did this happen?" She expected no answer to her questions. She didn't expect anything. But then in the distance, Sandy heard the Song Sparrow singing. "That can't be!" She rushed to the window and lifted it open, and the melody was repeated.

"This can't be!" she thought. *"Song Sparrows don't sing at this hour!"* Then Sandy quickly turned around to see if the Whisperer was sitting in the chair. Alas, the chair was empty...or so it seemed. "Are you here?" she asked aloud. No response was forthcoming. She looked about the small room and found nothing, but silence. Sadness overwhelmed her. She reached out to shut the window, and then, it happened. The Song Sparrow's melody touched her ear again.

Sandy returned to her chair and stared at the empty chair. "You are here! It's not my imagination. This is real!" Her first inclination was to call for Michael, but quickly realized that would disrupt what was happening. *"What should I do? How can I communicate with you?"*

Sandy felt desperate. She so wanted to connect with the Whisperer but had no idea how to do so. She took several deep breaths to calm herself, which served her well. Very quickly, she relaxed and simultaneously recalled the message from the self-help book. The memory was strong, and the message, written in Papyrus font, was so vivid that she could see it on the page as if it were right before her.

Listen to the Breath.
Listen to the Silence.
Simply be with the Silence.

Sandy's curious nature presumed the powerful recall that she experienced was a nudge to follow the guidance of the message. For a brief moment, she was apprehensive, but then she chose, as was suggested in the book, to open her heart to the situation. *"Don't listen to your suspicious mind, Sandy. This is an opportunity to rest in the Silence. The least that can happen is that you will have a restful moment. The most that can happen remains to be seen. Just embrace the opportunity."* And this she did. She listened to her breath, found a comfortable rhythm and then slipped into the Silence. The transition was so easy.

Time passed or so it seemed without Sandy's notice, until the early morning performance began. The Song Sparrow, who clearly had access to some type of high-tech microphone, was sharing her arias with the entire neighborhood. *"Ah. The tiny soprano with the large voice,"* thought Sandy. With her eyes still closed, she reached out to touch Michael and was surprised when her arm slipped off of her chair. Only then did she realize that she was still in her Sacred Space. Another surprise came when she found that the Sparrow's gig was right on time…dawn was unfolding.

Sandy couldn't believe that she had slept the entire night in her Sacred Space. She attempted to get out of her chair, but in so doing, her Journal and favorite pen fell to the floor. "Oh, dear," she muttered as she bent over to gather her writing materials. Once retrieved, Sandy noticed something strange. When the book fell from her lap, the pages naturally opened up to the last entry. That wasn't the strange part; it was not uncommon for a book to spread itself to the most recently used pages. What was odd left Sandy speechless. She stared at the last page, and then flipped through the previous pages. Then she returned to the empty chair and flipped through the pages again.

As she sat there clearly befuddled, a soft knock, so gentle in its intention came from the door. The tap was barely audible, but it managed to bring Sandy out of her stuporous state. Unable to articulate a response, she responded in thought. *"Michael, please come in."* He peeked in hoping that he was not intruding upon his wife's spiritual time. As he neared her chair, she began to weep.

"Dear One, what has happened?" He kneeled in front of her chair wanting to help his Beloved, but not knowing what type of assistance to offer. He placed one hand on hers, hoping that would be soothing and another on her thigh, hoping for the same outcome. He could see that the magic touch was doing what was needed.

"I'm so sorry, Michael." Sandy mumbled while trying to wipe the tears away with her shirt sleeve. "This is no way to greet you."

"Don't worry about me, Sandy. Please tell me what is going on."

She scooted out of her chair and joined Michael on the floor. He wrapped his arms around her and the energy shift was noticeable. The closeness enabled Sandy to breath normally again. Soon, a loud sigh was heard.

"Thank you for being here," she said in a depleted tone. Just whispering a few words seemed to exhaust her. Scanning the room, Michael noticed her water glass was empty.

"Sweetie, I think you are dehydrated. I'm going to get some water. Is that okay?" Initially she held him tighter, but then released him to go. His task was quick and efficient. He returned with water, orange juice, almonds, and blueberries.

"Wow!" Her voice was still minimal, but her eyes indicated interest. She immediately popped a few blueberries and then followed with several large swallows of water. Another sigh was released. She was perking up.

Optimistically, Michael again asked about the situation. Sandy was able to respond this time. "Please don't worry, I'm okay. I promise! I'm okay." Her words were reassuring, but didn't explain the circumstances. He attempted to be patient.

"You can chill on the patience, Dear, I'm just about ready to talk now." Sandy took several long deep breaths… it was helping. "I don't exactly know what is going on yet, Michael, but I'm almost certain that it's a good thing.

"Something happened yesterday before you came home that we didn't have time to discuss, but I need to update you on that before we talk about what just happened. Sandy quickly apprised her husband about her efforts to find greater understanding of the sunrise question that she had received. She elaborated on her journaling session and the unusual encounter she had with the Song Sparrow. While she spoke, they both nibbled on the nuts and enjoyed a glass of orange juice. By the time the update was completed Sandy was feeling stronger and more centered.

"So, last night I couldn't quiet my thoughts, so I came in here to distract myself. I wasn't planning on journaling, but then the craziest thing happened. Around midnight, I heard the Song Sparrow singing. It didn't make sense. But I went over to the window and raised it up to see if I had heard correctly. And sure enough, the Sparrow sang her melody again. Since the Whisperer was here the last time she sang, I thought maybe He/She had returned. I begged for a sign, and then, the Sparrow sang again. I chose to believe that was a sign. I was tickled, pleased, over the top, and frustrated that I didn't know how to communicate with the Whisperer. And then I remembered the message that we discussed about Simply being in the Silence, so I situated myself in my chair and took by deep breaths and then followed the instructions. Michael, that's all I remember.

"Then this morning, I was awakened by the Song Sparrow and found myself still here in this room. That was a surprise. And then, I found this!" Sandy grabbed her Journal, flipped the pages to yesterday's entry, and showed it to her husband.

"This is what I wrote yesterday, Mike." Then she turned to the next page and used her thumb to flip through numerous pages. "This wasn't here yesterday, Mike. But look at this! Look at all these pages written in my handwriting.

"I have no memory of doing this!"

Michael was as confused as his wife. He glanced through the pages, knowing full well that it was Sandy's handwriting. Now, he understood why she was so unsettled when he found her this morning. "Have you read this yet, Sandy?"

"No! I was contemplating it when you knocked on the door. I am bewildered, incredibly curious, and dancing with fear."

"May I make a suggestion?" asked Michael. Sandy nodded in agreement. "Let's relocate to the living room, where we can sit beside each other and read this together." Sandy was delighted to shift to their comfy sofa, but she was concerned about taking up Michael's time. Knowing what he was dealing with at work, she did not want to create chaos for him at home. She was about to say something when he replied to her concerns.

"Sandy, this is Saturday and we both have time to explore this unusual situation. I don't feel burdened by this; I feel excited. Let's make some egg tacos and enjoy them while we read what you wrote last night." Michael was a dream spouse. Considerate, caring, and loving. Once again, she was reminded how fortunate she was.

Michael addressed the tacos while Sandy brewed their favorite coffee and prepared the coffee table. Everything was nicely arranged and ready when the tacos were delivered. "These two are yours," he said pointing to the left of the plate.

"Hmm! This smells so good! How long has it been since we've had your delicious tacos?" Michael reminded her it was just the previous weekend and then suggested that they eat the first taco before they began to read the Journal.

"Works for me!" Each grabbed their preferred taco and took the first bite in unison. "Delicious! The best yet!" proclaimed Sandy.

"You always say that Dear! And it's true! These are the best yet!" They giggled playfully momentarily distracting themselves from the work ahead. "Okay, Girl, are you ready for this?" Michael sensed a bit of hesitation, but Sandy shook it off and nodded indicating that she was ready.

"Yes, I am ready and I'm grateful that you're here, Mike. Part of me is very excited to see what unfolds and another part of me is apprehensive. But that's okay because your presence gives me the courage to do this and I'm going to do it with an open heart." The couple shared a kiss fortifying their mutual courage.

Sandy reached over for the Journal and opened it to the first page of the unknown entry. As she looked at it, Michael suggested they begin with a deep breath. It was timely. He led with an elongated breath, and she followed. Her confidence returned. His admiration for Sandy expanded.

Sandy's eye attached to page. She paused for a moment as she allowed herself to absorb the first sentence.

"Dear Old Friend, so grateful am I to be in your presence once again. In truth, I am often with you, but to know that you are aware of my presence fills my heart with gratitude.

I ask, Dear Old Friend, that you listen with the ears of your heart. There is much that we must discuss, for The Time Is Now, and those who are called must rally to complete the tasks that each is intended to address. I approach you now, Old Friend, because the ache within you is evidence. Often you have wondered what your reason for being is and then the distractions of your plane drew you to other matters that captured your attention.

You have served well in many ways and your kindness has touched the hearts of many. All that you have done, Dear Old Friend, prepared you for the next phase of this existence. As said, Dear Friend, The Time Is Now!

In days ahead, you must return to your spiritual practice. Even though your current work is demanding, you must create time for the call that is your mission in this life experience. Fear not this request, for you are one who is exceptional at multi-tasking. You will find that the return to your spiritual path will enhance your life in countless ways. Your burdens will become Gifts, and your negative energy will shift in ways that are yet to be known. So many changes are coming, all of which will propel you forward into your Divine Work.

Already, you are content and pleased with your present life. Please hear me when I say the best is yet to come. Old Friend, so much more awaits you, and so needed you are. Yes, you heard correctly. You are needed! Dear Friend, you are here for a reason and the purpose of your being is coming into fruition. This is why you have been summoned.

You and your Beloved Spouse ponder why you are able to hear each other's thoughts. You laugh about it and frequently describe it as weird, and yet, the convenience of this type of communication intrigues you. You wonder why this has happened to you and you fear that others may discover your secret. This fear is a vulnerability that diminishes your power and your outreach. For this reason, the fear must be faced. The book recently read provides the guidance that will assist you in facing this fear. Dear Old

Friend, face this fear with an open heart and a curious mind.

Because you and Your Husband have grown accustomed to this way of communicating, you no longer perceive it as weird, until you think about how others might perceive you if they knew about your Gift. Perhaps, Dear Friend, you underestimate your Friends. Just as your Friend Jennifer admires you and wishes to learn about your skillset, so too may others. If you were to ponder about this more extensively, you may conclude that your fear not only inhibits you, but it also deprives others of the opportunity of being inspired by your Gift.

In essence, Dear Old Friend, your Gift is a memory of a time long past, when everyone communicated in this way. It was not weird; it was normal. The memory awakened within you and Michael for a reason. Ponder this please and seek within for the understanding that will be illuminated by your efforts.

Please rest for a moment, Dear Friend. You and your Spouse have consumed a great amount of information. A breath of fresh air would be restorative for both of you. Perhaps, the Friend Song Sparrow might bless you with another melody.

Sandy and Michael remained still, each trying to grasp what was happening. Both were excited and stunned, and each wanted to know more about the message that was so unusually received. Sandy eventually turned the Journal over on her lap and reached out for Michael's hand. The magic of touch grounded them and brought them back into the physical world. They leaned against each other, keenly appreciating the closeness and the experience they were sharing. Neither spoke nor heard the other's thoughts. They just sat in the Silence until the melodious Song Sparrow landed at the kitchen window and bellowed her wonderful morning greeting. The arrival of the operatic Song Sparrow shifted the couple's energy.

"Well, if that's not a sign, what is?" remarked Michael. "The amplification of her melody is extraordinary."

"She is an amazing little creature!" Sandy concurred. "As you can see and hear, this little one has been playing a major role in my life in recent hours."

"Yes, she certainly has!" He started to say more but Sandy posed the question that he was about to ask her.

"What do you make of this, Michael?"

"Well, I don't really know how to talk about it yet, Sandy. But I can tell you that I believe whatever is happening is real. As unusual as this may seem presently, I think it is the opportunity of a lifetime. How about you, Dear? How are you feeling about this? So far, the message is breathtaking and I'm eager to hear the rest of it." Michael's exuberance validated Sandy's thoughts. She was extremely grateful that they were having this experience together.

"My response is very similar to yours," she began. "Not only is the message itself beautifully presented, but it is also heartrending and brilliant. Obviously, the Whisperer knew in advance that you and I were going to read it together. How did She or He know that? It seems as if everything has been orchestrated, including the appearance of the lovely Song Sparrow. Mike, it all seems unbelievable; nevertheless, I believe it's real too."

Michael's tender way of approaching a conversation was just one of his many gifts. This particular aspect of his personality was one that Sandy really appreciated.

"Last night," he said softly, "you encouraged me to Simply Be in the Silence, which was exactly what I needed to hear." Looking into Sandy's eyes, he continued, "Well, maybe today, we should just Be with the Moment. We cannot expect ourselves to completely comprehend everything that is unfolding, but there is something that we can definitely do. We can give this moment all the attention it deserves."

A sigh of relief was barely audible. "Yes," replied his Beloved. "That's exactly what we can and should do!" With that said, the Songster validated the decision from a distant maple tree.

"So, let's replenish our coffee cups and get started!" Michael was in good spirits. Even though his situation at work was complicated, he managed to focus his attention upon Sandy's extraordinary incident. His excitement touched her heart. As he rushed to the kitchen to refill their coffee cups, she fell in love with him all over again. "What are you grinning about?" he asked while handing Sandy's cup to her.

"Nothing!" she replied. "Just loving you. That's all!"

"Hmm! That's a lot!" he replied to her reply. "Love you more!"

The lightheartedness bridged the way for the next viewing of the message. The couple settled comfortably on the sofa while Sandy retrieved the Journal and turned it upright. Once again, she was taken aback by the written material that she clearly wrote the night before. She took a long, deep breath and Michael did the same.

"Welcome back, Dear Friends. Once again, it is a pleasure to be in your company. As you took your deep breath, others from near and far joined with you. Many watch over you as you pursue this journey, and Everyone wishes that your journey is safe, productive, and meaningful.

As you read the words that you received last evening, you may find yourself hearing the words from within just as you do when you hear the thoughts of each other. The process is very similar. When you hear Michael's thoughts, it is as if you hear them from within you. This is also true when Michael hears your thoughts. Although you have no recall of last night's experience, the process was the same. As we sat across from one another, you heard my thoughts, and you carefully recorded all that was said. This transpired for a reason, Dear Old Friend.

Your heart has been aching for more meaning and it has been calling to you to listen. You listen to others with exceptional care. Even the Song Sparrow is heard by your remarkable listening skills. This is not a coincidence, Dear One. You have been primed for this since your arrival to this life experience. In days to come, you will remember incidents that happened in your past that indicated you were on the path to being a Listener. All transpired as was intended and now you have reached the moment that has been waited for throughout this lifetime, even though you had no idea that you were waiting for this. You have arrived, Dear Old Friend! And now, the work begins. Do not fear this reality...celebrate it! Your reason for being has revealed itself!

My Dear Friend, you have the privilege to receive messages that will be presented to the masses. Sometimes, the message will be delivered to someone nearby, others may be delivered to distant locations; however, most of your work will be intended to reach the masses. This is your mission, Dear Friend. A privilege it is to have this opportunity to serve in this way.

Although your listening skills on this plane are exemplary, an adjustment will be required for the upcoming work. This will transpire quickly as we continue working together as we did last night. You need not fear this process, it simply will unfold as we unite through the transmission process. What you are will become more and the work will proceed rapidly.

In days ahead, you will be invited to receive more messages from a variety of sources. Unlike last night, you will be awake during these sessions and aware of everything that transpires during our collaborative work. In essence we are a team with a mutual purpose. We need you to receive and present the intended messages of the moment and you need us to present the messages to you. As with all collaborations we must learn to work with each other. As you can see from the message before you, our task went well. The collaboration was a joyful event for those who assisted you, and we are eager to work with you again when you are consciously present so that you can share the joy of our endeavors.

Dear Old Friend, we have done similar work throughout many lifetimes. Although you currently have no memories of our previous experiences, suffice it to say we have shared many productive collaborations. We are a team of long-standing. We are Dear Old Friends.

Today, our work has already begun. By reading the message from last night you recognize that your purpose is one that demands an allocation of time. Finding balance in your new schedule requires careful consideration. Your health and wellness are a priority. Your relationship is a priority. Your current employment is a priority. Your purpose is a priority. As you can see your purpose has temporarily complicated your life. Breathe these priorities in and embrace the fullness of your life. Rest assured your heart will guide you.

Dear Friend, perhaps it is time for another consultation with your Beloved. Both of you will be affected by your new schedule. It is wise to be openhearted and patient when seeking balance with life's unfolding circumstances. Consideration of Loved Ones is essential."

Once again, Sandy and Michael nestled together. They sat quietly trying to absorb the impact of the message. Sandy's mind was whirling about attempting to create a plan that wouldn't create disruption for Michael. At the same time Michael was recognizing how much his job was affecting Sandy. The message intended for his Beloved was also a wakeup call for him. He too needed to review and adjust his schedule so that it accommodated their relationship.

"Michael, what are your thoughts about all of this?" Sandy was so absorbed in her own thoughts that she wasn't tuning into his.

151

"It's incredible, Sandy! You're receiving the most extraordinary information about your purpose in life. This is what people all over the world desire and long for...it's mind-boggling and it's real! I'm so happy for you. Sandy, witnessing your experience has also been a life-changing experience for me. I'm very grateful. What about you, Dear? I can't imagine the impact this is having on you."

Sandy tried to respond, but too many thoughts were whizzing about in her mind.

"Oh, dear mind of mine, please be still!"

"I heard that," her Beloved responded. "Let's take a few deep breaths together. That always calms us down." Michael's suggestion was on the mark.

"Thanks, Dear. As you can tell I'm a bit overwhelmed. The idea that I'll be learning how to receive these remarkable communiques blows my mind. My emotions are a roller coaster at the moment, but that will pass. As you said earlier, this is the opportunity of a lifetime, and I really want to make the most of this. There are flashes of self-doubt, but that will pass too, hopefully. As the Whisperer spoke of my readiness for this task, it felt right. I have been a listener all my life and it makes sense that my previous experiences would prepare me for this next step. I'm very excited!

"And I'm concerned about the impact this may have on our relationship, Michael. Trying to balance all of this is daunting."

"Don't worry, Sandy. We are going to make this work! Because you allowed me to be part of your experience, I've learned how much my job is already affecting our relationship. We both need to make some changes. Sandy, truly, I'm not worried about this. Just as the Whisperer described the multi-life relationships that you have shared, we too, you and I, are a good team. And we also are good friends who can and will make the necessary changes to live our lives fully."

Chapter Six

*M*ichael's pronouncement, stated with unshakeable confidence about the couple's ability to manage their work and social lives, empowered them both. Inspired by Sandy's riveting experience, he was ready to examine his issue at work that was just the day before feeling like a huge burden. His attitude had shifted. He was optimistic, self-assured, and eager to discover a healthy and inspiring solution to his teams' despondency. "I'm on this," he happily declared. "Thank you, Sandy. Your remarkable experience and our conversations last night and this morning have flipped a switch for me. I'm not afraid of this challenge anymore. In fact, I'm ready to get it done!" Sandy, relieved by Michael's renewed energy, applauded his turnaround.

"Wow!" she responded cheerfully. "Your enthusiasm inspires me, Mike! And I must say this aloud, even though my thoughts are probably blasting you with my waves of gratitude. "I'm so grateful. Your presence grounded me throughout this unusual event. I'm so, so grateful you were here. Your response to all of this helped me to accept it, believe it, and absorb it. I'm also glad that you accepted the information as a gift for yourself. That made the experience even more exceptional.

"So, thank you! Thank you! Thank you!"

"Amen!" Her Beloved replied. "Are you heading for your Sacred Space now, Sandy?"

"Yes, I am!" she was giddy with excitement. "Shall we join up later?"

Michael agreed to her suggestion and laughed. "I suspect our friendly Song Sparrow will let us know when it's time to reunite!" After sharing a big hug, each departed for their preferred room.

As Sandy entered her Sacred Space, there was a rush of anticipation, excitement, and hopefulness. It was breathtaking! Even though it had only been a few hours since she and Michael had relocated to this living room, it seemed like forever. *"I am so grateful to be here."* Before she sat down, Sandy observed the room. It was the same as before, and yet it felt different. The birds were happily enjoying their morning menu. The dust she had noticed on the writing table yesterday was still there waiting her attention. The Journal, which was not in its usual place, gave her a moment of angst before she realized it was in her hand. *"Ah, silly me,"* she thought remembering the reason for its absence. Bringing the Journal to her heart, Sandy embraced it with extreme fondness. *"We've had quite the experience in the last twenty-four hours. And I suspect today is also going to be very active."*

After giving the room one more glance, Sandy settled into her chair and took a deep breath as was her way. Then her eyes turned toward the empty chair. Her curiosity could not help but wonder if it was occupied. *"Are you there, my Dear Old Friend?"* Waiting hopefully, she remained silent, but busily scanned the room and listened for some type of response. Lightning did not strike, which she decided was a good thing. She looked about for a Song Sparrow, but none was to be seen, nor was a superfluous musical rendition noticed within her hearing range. *"Wishful thinking,"* she thought, and then opened her Journal to a fresh page.

As usual, she began with a notation of the day, date, and time, a habit of long standing. Another elongated breath was taken as she considered what her first entry would be. So much had happened, she didn't know where to begin. Then she boldly announced, "With an open heart and a curious mind, I begin today's journaling."

"Dear Journal of mine, I'm not certain how to begin today. As you well know, things have been a bit odd around here. I wonder what your experience was as I was receiving the information from the Whisperer. Did you notice a difference?" Sandy shook her head. "Jeepers! You're talking to your Journal as if it were alive. Get a grip, Girl! Just write about your experience!" Sandy did, as Sandy demanded.

"Okay! Dear Journal, lots has happened recently. I don't understand everything that has transpired, but I know it was real and I want it to continue. Communication occurred with another that I referred to as the Whisperer. This communique was unbelievable, and yet, I am certain it was real. I want to connect with the Whisperer again, but I'm not sure how to do that. If we did it before, then

we can do it again. Please, please, please, let it happen again." Sandy's desire for connection was understandable. Her appeal for connection deeply touched the hearts of those who were near.

"*Greetings, Dear Old Friend, be in peace! Your appeal for connection was heard and We, who are your assistants, are delighted to be in your presence.*" Sandy's sigh of relief was audible. She started to speak again but was not clear what was best.

"Do I address you with my thoughts, or should I use my audible voice?" No response was heard, so Sandy grabbed her pen and readied herself for another unspoken message. She was wise to do so, for once the pen was in hand, she heard the voice within.

"*Dear Friend, let us speak of this. We can hear both your spoken words and your unspoken words. Please remember that when you attempt to communicate with us, we do receive your message. During these early stages of our re-connection, we urge you to have your Journal and pen ready to record everything that is said. This process will train you for what is coming. By recording our discussions, you will reclaim a skillset that prepares you for the upcoming work that awaits you. Furthermore, by recording your words and our words, you create a memoir that will serve as a resource for the future. Many conversations we will have, Old Friend. Because of this, you will at times feel overloaded with information. There will be times when you may wish to review something that was said, and your daily writings will be there for you. There will also be times when you wish to share a message with a particular person or with numerous people, and you will retrieve the message from the memoirs that you have created from our many conversations. Suffice it to say, this process is multi-purposeful. You are given the opportunity to practice receiving messages, and you will have the pleasure of sharing these messages as is desired and needed.*

Yes, Dear Friend, you heard correctly. Many of the messages that you receive are intended to be shared and some are intended to reach the masses. Perhaps that idea causes you unrest. If it does, be assured you are not the first who has responded in this manner. One is amazed and overwhelmed when this process unfolds. One is challenged when they realize the messages are to be presented to others. In that moment one is faced with the reality that having this incredible Gift draws attention, and one wonders what the attention will bring.

Look before you, Dear Old Friend. Are not these words, which you see before you, proof that this encounter is real? Hearing an unseen voice can be perceived as a Gift or it can be perceived as a complication. In truth, it can be and often is both. Particularly in the early phase of one's introduction to this reality. Some will believe your story of this unusual experience and others will not. You were most fortunate that your Beloved was near and both able and willing to validate your experience. As you well know, that was not a coincidence. The reassurance you received from your Spouse was comforting and it assisted you in a moment when you were overwhelmed by the magnitude of this event. His presence was intended, and this you well know.

What is most important, Dear Old Friend, is that you trust yourself. In the days ahead, you will have many more so-called unusual experiences. At times you may doubt yourself, and then your thoughts may exacerbate your doubts. This is unfortunate, but it is not uncommon. It is simply part of the human condition. When this happens, remember what you have received. Reread the messages if necessary! Remind yourself of the goodness that you have received and been privileged to chronicle.

Old Friend, we speak of these possibilities so that you will not be surprised if it happens. Please trust yourself as we trust you. If you find yourself deeply concerned or worried about an issue, remember we are here to assist you. Please do not forget this!

Take a break, Dear Friend. You need time to consume this information."

Sandy placed her pen down. The Whisperer was correct. She did need time to adjust to this new reality that was being presented to her. It seemed unbelievable and at the same time, she knew that it was intended. In some ways, it felt as if she had just accepted a new job for which she didn't remember applying. It was a strange feeling, but at this point, strange events were becoming commonplace. Sandy wondered how she would work this new job into her daily schedule, and then, she just accepted it for what it was. *"It's unrealistic to think that you're going to have all the answers laid out in front of you. Just take this one day at a time and all will be well."* Noticing that her thought had asserted a wise and agreeable decision, Sandy was prepared to continue. Uncertain how to make her preference known, she looked at the empty chair and simply said, "Hello! Are you there? I'm ready to continue, if you are."

"Indeed! I am most grateful for your rapid return. Do you have any questions regarding our conversation thus far?"

"At this point, I have hundreds of questions, none of which really needs to be answered at this time. Although there are no words to express my current state of being, I simply know that what is happening is happening for a reason. As you have said, I am here to receive the messages, and you are here to deliver them to me. How the work will be presented to the world is information that will be provided when the time comes. I think that accurately sizes things up." Sandy paused briefly and then quickly asked a question.

"Is it possible for me to know your name?" As Sandy asked the question, she surprisingly realized that the Whisperer had not spoken her name. "You kindly refer to me as a Dear Old Friend, which certainly warms my heart, but how do I return your kindness? What is your preference? How may I address you so that you feel equally honored?" A brief pause that seemed like an hour to Sandy passed before a response was heard.

"Your concern for my well-being touches my heart deeply. An explanation is deserved. Dear Old Friend, as said before, you and I have been Friends throughout the ages. We have known each other by many different names. Over time, a decision was made to create a solution that addressed all names and all times. This is why you are referred to as Dear Old Friend, because you are, always

*have been, and always will be my Dear Old Friend.
Likewise, I have the privileged of being addressed in the
same manner. As are you my Dear Old Friend, so too am
I to you.*

*"When you need me, simply call out, Dear Old Friend,
and I will be present."* The tender moment was felt by both
Old Friends and by many others who also witnessed the
exchange.

"Once again, your kindness unsettles me." Sandy
struggled to maintain some sense of composure. "Perhaps,
I am not accustomed to this depth of emotion."

"Perhaps," replied the Dear Old Friend, *"it is difficult
for you to receive the Love that is being transmitted towards
you in this moment of deep connection. The power of this
energy can seem overwhelming, and unfortunately, it also
can be misinterpreted. So, let us take advantage of this
precious moment and simply be with the expansive energy
that is being sent to you at this time. This is the energy of
Love that activates All that exist within the Great Existence
and beyond."*

Sandy sat quietly and envisioned her Dear Old Friend
in a similar position. It was difficult to understand the
depth of Love that she was feeling, but she recognized the
importance of becoming comfortable with this reality. *"If
only others could feel what I am experiencing now, what a
different world we would be living in."*

Turning to the empty chair, Sandy stared at it as if she
could actually see her invisible friend. "This is the way
everyone is supposed to feel, isn't it?"

"Yes." The response, barely a whisper, was sufficiently heard.

"Well, this is an endeavor worth addressing. It's a sad statement when one says to another that their kindness is unsettling. Dear Old Friend, it is definitely worth my time and energy to learn how to embrace the Love that I just experienced."

Sandy resumed her position enjoying the comings and goings of the backyard birds, squirrels, rabbits, and the unknown visitors who managed to avoid the human eye. "Look at all of you! What great beauty you bring to my life, and to many others, I'm sure." Without notice, Sandy slipped into a lovely, relaxed state.

Her Dear Old Friend, watching her from the empty chair, was pleased. Sandy was becoming more comfortable with the so-called unusual experience. This was a very good sign. There was much work that awaited them.

Chapter Seven

"**S**hall we begin, Old Friend? Shall we tackle the work that awaits us?" The questions posed by Sandy delighted her Dear Old Friend.

"Ah, you have successfully heard my thoughts. This is very good, Old Friend! You progress rapidly and this will propel our work forward." The positive feedback thrilled Sandy. She was one that enjoyed learning new things, working hard, and making rapid progress. Her Companion's words were music to her ears.

"Old Friend, your enthusiasm pleases us. Let us begin our work with an exploration of your curious mind. As you have already learned, when the curious mind is working with you, your work proceeds easily; however, when the focus of the curious mind goes elsewhere, the work can become sluggish and frustrating. The more aware you are of the activities of your mind, the more able you are to manage its productivity. In truth if you are not paying attention to your mind's focus, you may find yourself in a predicament. For this reason, we wish to remind you of

suggestions that were provided in the Self-Help Book that you shared with your Spouse and Friend Jennifer.

When receiving messages, your mind must be focused upon that process. If it begins to wander, you must be aware that this is happening, which means you must be consciously present. Consistency is the goal; however, the reality is that the mind is inclined to seek other opportunities occasionally. Unfortunately, such behavior can quickly expand to a lengthy absence from the intended work. In order to control the meandering mind, one is wise to follow this suggestion:

> *'Be patient, be kind, and be compassionate*
> *with yourself and with your mind.*
> *Remember, your mind is a part of you.*
> *Treat the mind in the same manner*
> *that you would like to be treated.'*

Dear Old Friend, another factor in our collaborative work that is wise to discuss is the relationship that develops among you and those who assist you. Just as your mind naturally prefers to be in charge of your relationship, so too will you naturally wish to be in charge in our relationship. This tendency can complicate our ability to work rapidly, because in this work situation, we have very different tasks. You are here to receive the messages, and we are here to present them to you.

Because the human mind so delights in creating its own path, it sometimes forgets that the messages received are not in the process of being created. They are already as they are intended to be. This misunderstanding can muddle our efforts. So, Dear Old Friend, please consider this suggestion as a gentle reminder. If we seem to be bogged down for whatever reason, it is best to avoid frustration by simply taking a moment to rest allowing everyone involved to breathe freely while expressing gratitude for this remarkable privilege that we share. In essence, Old Friend, this suggestion is one that is wise to carry in your heart at all times...a reminder that Life is a privilege to share."

"Thank you for this time together," whispered Sandy. "You remind me of how important it is to be a good listener. Your suggestions are words of wisdom that should indeed be carried in my heart at all times. Now I understand why it is so important to take notes of our conversations. This one will definitely be highlighted so that I can quickly access it. Dear Friend, this has been most helpful. Shall we continue?

"No!" Sandy quickly asserted. "Before we move forward," she spoke to the seemingly empty chair, "I wish to express my gratitude to you, Dear Old Friend, and to all the other Old Friends who are also present. I am so grateful to be part of this collaboration." As Sandy envisioned other Companions gathered in her small room, she worried about the lack of space and the looming dust on the writing table that still had not been addressed. She felt very small and very grateful as she sat in her room of infinity.

"We too are grateful, Old Friend! We are most excited about working with you again. Do not worry about accommodating us. Your room without walls provides ample space for all who wish to be of assistance. It is most

167

pleasurable to be in your company. Long we have waited for this moment."

Sandy so enjoyed the company of these unseen Friends. She wondered about their perspective of this new relationship. How long have they been waiting for this reunion. Why now? What makes this the right time? So many questions. She envisioned sitting in her Sacred Space with the visible Dear Old Friend talking endlessly about everything. Reminiscing about the past and speaking of what is yet to be. How wonderful it would be to stay up into the wee hours of the morning discussing All That Is with this Dear Old Friend.

"Yes, Dear One, that would be most delightful. And in truth, your dream will be actualized through our communiques. We will speak of what was, what is, and what will be, and these messages will be shared with the peoples of Earth.

"As you can see, Dear Friend, your assistance is needed. What is known must be shared and it must be done with the utmost care. We are here to assist the peoples of Earth with their evolutionary development. To do so, we must be certain that the messages are presented as they were intended. This is your role, Dear Friend. As the Listener, it is your privilege and your responsibility to receive each word as it was spoken. You are not here to edit or to alter the messages that you receive. Great care was given these messages when they were created, for they are the answers for the future of Mother Earth's wellness and for all the inhabitants that call her Home.

"Many are here to assist you, Old Friend. Do not presume that the burden of this role is solely yours. As

said, many are here who have worked on this mission for ages. All involved accept responsibility for this Mission of Mercy. You are not alone, Dear Friend. Our desire is that you understand and accept the importance of this mission. Your assistance is needed! Those, who are here to assist you, grasp the overwhelming sense of responsibility that comes with this new assignment. Therefore, we stand by you now to affirm your capability for this mission and to reassure you that you are never alone. We are many, and we are One, and together the Mission of Mercy sustains itself.

"Our mission is expansive, and it is necessary. As you well know, the Life Being Earth is under great stress. Her health is of great concern to all who inhabit the Great Existence. The primary intention of the Mission of Mercy is to rescue Mother Earth from her current situation. While she valiantly continues serving and caring for all her residents, her fellow Life Beings, the extraordinary efforts that she makes on their behalf are not reciprocated.

"In days of old, the initial inhabitants lived in alignment with the Earth's needs. They graciously accepted her gifts and lived harmoniously with each other and with the land and the waters that were provided. Then the new species arrived. Those who were honorable respected the bounty of the planet. They too graciously accepted her gifts while treading carefully upon the land. These kind ones lived upon the Earth honoring and caring for the planet without causing her harm.

"Then another type of the new species came upon the scene. Their behaviors were different. Their desires morphed

169

---

in ways that were not conducive to living with others. They became problematic. Their new way of being interfered with the existing inhabitants including the courteous ones of their own species. The newcomers misunderstood the ways and the importance of the Life Beings previously on the planet. They considered these Beings to be less than their own species, and they erroneously presumed to have ownership of all lands, waters, and species upon the planet. Mother Earth initially perceived this unruly species as innocent children who simply needed time to mature into the better people they were intended to be. As a Mother she demonstrated great patience and kindness as the humans continued to behave disrespectfully towards her and other species with whom they coexisted. Their unacceptable behavior spread as they grew in population and expanded across all her continents. In each setting that was occupied, more harm than good was initiated.

"Those from afar who observed this evolutionary mishap grew more and more concerned about the planet Earth. Attempts were made to improve the situation, but it became increasingly evident that the misguided ways of the species were ingrained within their developmental system.

"What is needed to rectify what has happened has to come from within the species themselves. They must accept their ill-fated destiny that is driven by their personal ill will. Although evidence of humankind's violent nature is widely known, few individuals would accept the idea that she or he suffered from ill will. They would agree that there is too much violence, but they would not agree that they were in any way part of the problem. The naiveté of the human *species is alarming. Because their species matured with the misunderstanding that they were more important than other species, they cannot accept that they are a carrier of ill will. The idea, which is true, is unbelievable to them. Even more unsettling is that many humans believe that within the human species there are some who are flawed while others are not.*

"Trying to convince people who developed believing a misunderstanding about their status within a community is not an easy task. They are not inclined to hear the truth from another. This is why the people of Earth must find the truth within, or they will find themselves in the most precarious situation.

"Dear One, as you receive these messages, you will wonder about your own wellness, just as the Readers of these messages will wonder about their wellness. This is intended! Wonder about your wellness! Ask yourself the hard questions that must be pursued to discover the ill will that exists within you.

"Old Friend, as the receiver of these messages, you must experience the truth of what is received. Ill will exists among the people of planet Earth. Although it is difficult to accept such a statement, it is true. Even though no one wants to believe this truth, it remains true. In essence, ill will is as toxic as any terminal illness. If it were professionally diagnosed as a terminal illness, great efforts would be made by humankind to cure the problem. This is the reaction that is desperately needed!

"When the human species grasps a difficult situation, they are tenacious in their efforts to improve the situation. To

*overcome ill will, the good people of Earth must accept that
it exists. Eventually, scientists and medical professionals
will speak of this truth, and their research will validate
the truth, but it will not cure the situation. Time is of the
essence. Altering the course of ill will comes from within. It
demands that every person accept responsibility for doing
their own personal research.*

*"Dear Old Friend, as you received the last statement,
what thoughts came to mind? Please take time to investigate
the thoughts that quickly came to mind."*

"My thoughts were many and quite frankly, it is
embarrassing to reveal them. My first reaction was to the
word 'demand.' I felt myself recoil to the idea that someone
thought they had the right to demand me to do something.
It felt like a huffy, arrogant reaction, a 'how dare you'
reaction. And then, my frame of thought quickly changed
to thinking about others' reaction. My attitude was aloof,
doubtful and judgmental. My thoughts were: do your really
think that people are going to do this? Do you really think
that people will acknowledge that they have ill will? As
you can see, my focus shifted from me and attached to
others. And shamefully, I admit that my attitude towards
the others' presumed reactions was unkind.

"This was a very important exercise for me. I witnessed
how quickly and cleverly my focus turned towards others
rather than accepting responsibility for my own self-
exploration. Obviously, this is unpleasant to acknowledge,
and at the same time, I am very grateful for this learning
experience. I witnessed my resistance to explore my own

behavior. And I also witnessed how quickly I focused on the possible flaws of others.

"Once again, I am experiencing the influence of the Self-Help book. One must be patient, kind, and compassionate when doing this inner work. This is a necessary component when exploring one's ill will, not only for yourself, but also for those whom you shift your ill will towards. The good news is that I did grasp what happened. To avoid looking at my own ill will, I turned my eyes to the assumed ill will of others. Through this experience, I noticed my ill will in action.

"My Dear Old Friends, how quickly we can learn about the ill will within us. While this incident was small and brief, it was evidence that ill will exists whether we want to believe it or not. This exercise has brought greater clarity to me. I do believe that ill will does exist. And yes, it definitely demands our attention."

"Well done, Old Friend! You successfully addressed your ill will by simply observing the thoughts of your mind. Your willingness to do this is noteworthy. Please remember the action that was taken because it is an essential factor in altering the course of ill will. Because you willingly chose to pause and seriously scrutinize your thoughts, you discovered more information about you and your thoughts. Had you not chosen to participate in this experience, your mind would have continued its rhetoric until it tired itself out. In the meantime, the negative, judgmental energy that you were producing would have continued to impact you and those around you, including Mother Earth.

"More must be said about your willingness to face your ill will. Our biggest hurdle in dealing with this tragic situation is fear. Unfortunately, fear is fearsome, and facing one's fear is not easy for most people. We speak of this so that you and all that you touch will understand that you are not alone.

"Open your heart, Dear Friend. Take several deep breaths and let us simply be together. As the Readers of your book will do this exercise, so too must you. Imagine them now. Readers across the globe taking advantage of a few moments of silence, all desiring to understand more about the ill will that resides within them. Each of you has your own work to do; however, each of you can send thoughts of good will to all those who join you in this moment of self-exploration and expansion.

…Breathe…

"Take another deep breath and as you slowly exhale send blessings and thoughts of good will to those who are also willingly participating in this exercise. Remember you are not alone. Here in this expansive community of other Readers, you share a mutual desire to learn more about who you are and who you desire to be.

"Continue to take your restorative deep breaths until you have found the pace and rhythm that are right for you. Embrace this opportunity to discover more about you. Yes, Dear Old Friend, you are the center of attention. Please monitor your thoughts along the way, so that the focus

remains upon you. Observe your thoughts because they are an extraordinary source of information.

"During this time, you may encounter surprises, disappointments, and much more. Whatever unfolds, simply be with the moment. You are gathering information about you. Some details will please you; others may not. Regardless of what surfaces, treat the discovery, the information about You, with kindness and compassion and accept the information as an opportunity for personal improvement.

"Let us begin, Dear Ones, with this statement. Whoever you are, wherever you are, the time is now! Please hear the message within this small statement.

Whoever you are, wherever
you are, the time is now!

"A message of extreme importance awaits you. As you read the message, please do so with an open heart. So many times have we attempted to inform you of your precarious situation, but unfortunately, our efforts have not been successful.

"The time is now! We come again to apprise you of your situation. Dear Peoples of the Earth, please hear these words. Your planet is in a serious crisis that demands your attention. As a creative species you have the ability to alter her current decline. This information about the Earth's declining health has been presented to you many times, but our warnings have been disregarded. Even now, when global awareness is higher than ever before, the vast

majority of your people remain in a stuporous state of denial.

"The magnitude of this crisis has caused the masses to fall into a paralysis of fear. Your fear is understood. We are fearful for you, not because you are incapable of the task before you, but because you are ignoring that which is blatantly obvious.

"Dear Ones, you are not alone! We repeat this message because it is true. Many are here to assist you, and we begin by speaking the truth of your circumstances. While the immensity of this task seems undoable that is not the case. Old Friends, your ability to address the pragmatic components of this crisis is already in place, and new possibilities are coming forward more rapidly than one can imagine. However, these strategic matters are not the primary issue.

"We have spoken of the predominant issue before; nevertheless, it is so important that it must be done again. Open your hearts to this truth, Dear Friends. The primary reason for Earth's decline is the negative energy that is created and dispersed by the human species. We understand that you may be bewildered by this concept, but it is the truth! This is where your efforts as a Global Community must focus.

"Because of the hostile nature of your species, many of you will resist accepting this as true. Although you may quickly accept this truth in others and blame these others as being 'the problem,' this erroneous conclusion will not resolve your crisis. Targeting others as the problem is an arrogant and foolish attitude that will only worsen your situation.

"Everyone is involved in this tragic situation, and everyone must be involved in the healing process that is necessary for Mother Earth. We speak not of the pragmatic actions that must be taken on her behalf, but of the acts of kindness that once existed within humans, and which must be reignited for the sake of humanity.

"Kindness can and will heal the Earth! This can happen quickly, if the people of Earth will actively participate in cleansing the negative behavior that brews within them. Please reread the previous sentence and bear witness to your thoughts. Make notes of everything that just raced through your mind.

- *What thoughts were positive, hopeful, and optimistic?*
- *What thoughts were founded in negativity, begrudging, denial, and blaming of others?*
- *Study what you observed so that you know the truth about yourself. And remember, you are not alone in this moment of self-discovery. Everyone who openly and honestly looks within will find something about themselves that needs improvement.*
- *Do not shame or blame yourself, and do not shame or blame others.*
- *Accepting one's own flaws is a sign of courage and strength, which prepares you for the next growth experience.*

"You must first accept the reality that ill will exists within you before you can alter it. If you begrudge the idea and turn your back on this reality, then you will continue to harm

yourself, others, and the Earth with your negative energy. On the other hand, if you accept the truth, you can quickly turn this ill-fated attitude around. It is so much easier to be kind than it is to be burdened by the weight of negativity.

Kindness heals!
Kindness begets kindness!
Kindness spreads rapidly!

"When kindness is shared, positive energy propels forward brightening the energy of others, including Mother Earth. The quickest most effective way of addressing the Earth's health crisis depends upon the cooperation of humanity. It relies upon the human species agreeing to alter the negative energy within their species.

"We can do this! We can choose to be people of kindness rather than people of anger, hatred, and violence. It is a choice that each person can choose. If we choose kindness over hostility, the reduction in negative energy that is currently bombarding the Earth could give the planet time to rest and to recuperate. During this reprieve, the pragmatic efforts that must be addressed can be managed.

"Dear Friends, please listen to the truth! Read the previous paragraphs again and accept the truth of your own participation in Earth's health situation and choose to do the right thing. Envision your own acts of kindness positively affecting those around you. See the contributions that you are making and the good will that you are spreading. See this happening within your mind and choose to make it a reality in your life.

"Choose to be a person of kindness, and in so doing, save the Earth.

…Breathe…

"Engaging with this topic is not easy. How could it be? Regardless of where or how you initially received the tragic message about the Earth, the truth is that it is hard to be with this heartbreaking information.

"Have compassion for yourself. Have compassion for the other Readers of this book. Have compassion for all the other folks who also are aware of the Earth's crisis. Have compassion for all those who are unaware or in denial of the Earth's situation. Have compassion for Mother Earth.

"Oh, Dear Friends, have hope! There is reason for hope. You, the people of Earth are the reason for hope. Yes, please read these words with the eyes of your heart and accept what is said as another truth that demands your attention.

"Were there not hope, this book would not have been prepared and presented to those who are in need. Were there not hope, all the other messages delivered to people across the globe would not have happened. Were there not hope, all the efforts made on behalf of the Earth would not have happened. Were there not an answer to this crisis situation, we would not have contacted you.

*"Through this small and simple chapter, you have learned that there is a way to resolve the Earth's health crisis. **You are the Answer!** Yes, Dear Friend, you and all*

your human Brothers and Sisters are the answer. Is this not Sweet Beauty?

"*You have the privilege of restoring Earth back to good health. By releasing your ill will and replacing that negative energy with the positive energy of good will, you have the means of revitalizing Earth's health. By improving your behaviors from ill will to good will and by embracing acts of kindness and sharing them with all you encounter, not only will you save the Earth from her current crisis, but you will also personally benefit from the changes made.*

"*Just as the Earth's health improves, so too will yours and all others' who reside on the planet. The changes that will occur on Mother Earth because of your willingness to better yourself will change the Earth as you now know it.*

"*Dear Friends, please open your hearts to the message that has been presented to you. Ponder it! Accept the reality that Mother Earth is in need. She deserves our help. She has given so much to us and never asked for anything in return. We have unfortunately taken her for granted. And even now when She is in ill health, She makes no request of us. She continues to provide for us as best She can. It is time for us to return her kindness and her immeasurable generosity.*

"*We have the means to restore her to good health. Each and every one of us has the ability to be kind to her, to praise her, to nourish her, to love her, to cherish her. We have the ability to do these simple tasks for her, and these acts of kindness will improve her health. By participating in these small acts of good will, the Earth will have time to rejuvenate from her crisis. During this time of recovery, the necessary sustainable projects that will stabilize and enhance her physical health can be implemented.*

"Everyone has a role to play. Underlying all efforts that are done are her behalf, the gestures of kindness and good will are the critical components that will revitalize her health.

"Dear Friends, you are the answer! By joining together as a Global Community and becoming the Family that you are intended to be, you will heal yourselves as you heal the Earth."

Part Three

Saving the Earth by Being the Better Person You are Intended to Be

Seeking Closure

Dear Readers,

Thank you for reading *The Power of Thoughts* and more importantly, thank you for opening your heart to the message presented throughout this book. As you may remember, I, the so-called author of this project, was reluctant to be involved with a Self-Help book. Too many were read during my years as a Psychotherapist, or so I thought. Now that we have reached this stage of the book, I see the beauty of what has transpired before my eyes. Once again, I am amazed by the process, grateful for being part of the process, and bewildered by the benevolence that facilitates the process.

The point of the Self-Help book was to prepare us, the Readers, for what is coming by educating us to the power of our thoughts. We discovered through the exercises provided that we are remarkable beings blessed with an exceptionally active mind that needs guidance. As the possessor of this remarkable asset, each of us is accountable for monitoring our own mind so that we are aware of its activities at all times. Because the human mind is multi-talented, it is capable of cogitating numerous thoughts at the same time with or without our conscious presence.

Hopefully, Dear Readers, you acquired more information about your mind and recognized just how clever it can be. Truthfully, this remarkable mind that we each have often thinks without our notice and these thoughts affect us whether we are aware of it or not. Common sense tells us that it is in our best interest to know what our mind is up to. It is also wise to know what you are up to.

In discovering more about one's mind, you also learn more about yourself. Who are you, Dear Friend? And who are you intended to be? Through conversations with others who also are seeking to know more about themselves, you will gain more and more knowledge about the Self you are truly intended to be. Also, you will learn more about the ill will that exists within you and within others, and your perspective of the world will change.

Once you become aware of ill will, you will see the futility of it, and you will notice when it activates within you. You will recognize it in others as well. However, rather than judging another person's ill will, instead observe what is transpiring within you and learn how this person's ill will affects you. Once experienced, inwardly express gratitude for the lesson and wisely release the negative energy that you endured. Then, the next step of this learning experience is to REMEMBER that you witnessed an act of ill will. The behavior witnessed is not to be mimicked. In essence, you have been shown how NOT to behave. If by chance, you have seen a similar behavior in yourself before, praise yourself for admitting it, and do the necessary work to reject that type of posturing from your array of behaviors.

Dear Readers, we all have work to do. Have compassion for yourself and have compassion for everyone else. We are all a work in progress. Patience, kindness, and compassion will serve us well during this transformative experience.

As we practice the suggestion in the previous paragraph, let us review what was learned from the brief fictional story. The most prominent factor that was demonstrated throughout the story was kindness. Each character regardless of his or her emotional situation was gentle, thoughtful, and kind. The story was presented in this way for a reason. This amiable manner of living life is noteworthy. The encounters were intense, emotional, and beneficial. There was no need for drama or chaos for the conversations were satisfying as they were. What was demonstrated was exceptional active listening, focused attention, kindness, and sincere tender care. In each situation, the needs of the participants were met with loving-kindness.

Dear Friends, this model of relational connection is not a fantasy; it is a choice, and it is a choice that is preferable to the examples that are provided through movies, television, and the internet. In a world that is bombarded by outrageous examples of human connections, we must remember that there are alternatives to these poor representations. Human decency demands that we seek a better way of engaging with one another. Our family units need to be founded in love and respect. Our relationships with others need to be openhearted and openminded, and diversity should be embraced and respected for the gift that it is. We are all Brothers and Sisters and it is time to accept this truth.

Unfortunately, behaviors of ill will are prominent in our daily lives, and worse yet, these behaviors have become models for generations. It will not be easy to shift to another way of being, but all who do will find life so much easier to live. Everyone will benefit. As one makes a positive change, another will follow, and eventually the masses will create a new model of living, which honors everyone equally, including Mother Earth and all her other species who also deserve a peaceful way of living.

Dear Readers, please give these thoughts consideration. They are more than just wishful thinking; they are possibilities that we are capable of creating. We need to make changes. Our present course is no longer viable. Mother Earth cannot continue bearing the ill will of our species, and we cannot continue without Her unbelievable generosity. This is our reality. We need to change.

On behalf of Mother Earth and all who live upon her, please choose to be the better person, the beautiful person, you are intended to be.

...In Peace Be...

All books can be easily purchased through:

The Center for Peaceful Transitions
www.centerforpeacefultransitions.com

Balboa Press
www.balboapress.com

Amazon.com
www.amazon.com

About the Author

As you read this book and others presented by Claudia Helt, the purpose of her role will become clear. Claudia's personal life has been one of ordinary circumstances. She grew up in a small town, attended university attaining two degrees in Psychology, and then enjoyed over three decades working as a psychotherapist. Her curious mind also led her to explore other healing modalities where she found another career as a Reiki Master.

She was, as you might imagine, initially taken aback when she began hearing a Voice of an unseen Presence. For her, the manner in which she receives these communiques is as mysterious as the material itself; however, after two and half decades of participating in this process, she now simply accepts these experiences as cherished connections for which she is eternally grateful.

Even after all these years her commitment to this collaborative process remains firm, and she intends to continue sharing future communiques as she is invited and guided.

Printed in the United States
by Baker & Taylor Publisher Services